MUSEUM
OF FINE ARTS
BOSTON

GREAT MUSEUMS OF THE WORLD

MUSEUM OF FINE ARTS
BOSTON

Paul Hamlyn LONDON · NEW YORK · SYDNEY · TORONTO

GREAT MUSEUMS OF THE WORLD

Foreword by
Perry Townsend Rathbone

Introduction by
Jan Fontein

Texts of this volume by
Adolph S. Cavallo
Jan Fontein
Gian Lorenzo Mellini
Pratapaditya Pal
Perry Townsend Rathbone
Henry H. Schnabel
William Stevenson Smith
Hanns Swarzenski
Cornelius Vermeule

Design by
Fiorenzo Giorgi

Originally published in Italian by
Arnoldo Mondadori Editore, Milan
ISBN 0 600 35923 9
© 1969-Arnoldo Mondadori Editore-CEAM-Milan
© 1969-Photographs Copyright by Kodansha Ltd.-Tokyo
This edition copyright © 1970 The Hamlyn Publishing Group Limited
London/New York/Sydney/Toronto
Hamlyn House, Feltham, Middlesex, England
All rights reserved
Printed and bound by Officine Grafiche Arnoldo Mondadori, Verona

FOREWORD

PERRY TOWNSEND RATHBONE
Director, Museum of Fine Arts, Boston

In the middle of the nineteenth century, Boston was the intellectual center of the yet to be completed United States. Boston published the books, set the intellectual tone, and combined thriving commerce with a leisurely but committed pursuit of spiritual and cultural values. What certainly must have irked the favored Bostonian as he returned from his travels to the European capitals was the lack in Boston of a properly constituted museum, or even a regularly organized symphony orchestra. Both those shortcomings were to be overcome as the century entered its final quarter.

On February 4, 1870, the Massachusetts Legislature granted a charter to a board of trustees, and the city provided a plot of land in the newly filled Back Bay, facing on what later became Copley Square. The nucleus of the new Museum was provided by the owners of several collections of art who desired to make them generally available to the public in a central place. Harvard wished to show its engravings; the Massachusetts Institute of Technology, its architectural casts; the Boston Athenaeum, its paintings, sculpture, and other objects; and the City of Boston, its most famous historic portraits.

Thus encouraged, the Museum began immediately a life of its own; while it started that very year to collect, to organize exhibitions, raise money, and execute all the things expected of the almost indefinable institution called a museum, it was not until July 4, 1876, that the infant Museum opened the doors of its first building on Copley Square. Thus it matched its own celebrations with the centennial of the nation's birth — a moment in time marked also by news dispatches on "Custer's Last Stand" in the West.

In those brave and far-off days, there was no income tax. Men of position could think big and act big. The Museum Trustees did. Twenty-two years after they opened the doors, the need for a new building was apparent. They purchased twelve acres in the Back Bay Fens, and set off in committee to study all the museums in Europe, a project that occupied them for three months and produced a 200-page report on the ideal museum. The perspective rendering of the new Museum shows the building covering the entire twelve-acre site. Here was a building a little short of the Louvre in size, to be financed entirely by private resources.

The style followed the prevailing Classical mode, and so it was through a Greek portal that the first visitors entered the new Museum in November, 1909. Sweeping vistas, ceremonial stairways, dramatic domes, and more columns awaited them within. Such expansive architecture today is unthinkable, but one cannot deny the grateful reflection that such grandiose American expressions stand a better chance of being preserved in the country's museums than in its railroad stations.

Six months were required to move the collections to the new building; among them were some of the greatest treasures in the Museum today. Even by that early date the primacy of the Museum in certain fields had already been established. Most conspicuous were surely the Oriental collections, already beyond compare in the world. Here the intellectualism of Boston was brought to bear on the Museum. Edward S. Morse, a self-taught Maine zoologist working in Salem, Mass., ventured out to Japan in 1877, one year after the Museum opened its doors, in search of brachiopods. He stayed to find, appreciate, and collect the historic art of Japan in concert with his fellow townsman, Ernest Fenollosa, and another Boston friend, Dr. William

Sturgis Bigelow. Together they literally uncovered a new world, one unknown to the West and half forgotten and even scorned by the Japanese themselves. The well-nigh incredible story of their quest is described in the following Introduction. Suffice it to say here, as an example of their contribution to the Museum, that their insight and devotion secured almost four-fifths of the five thousand Japanese and Chinese paintings now in the Boston collection.

This redoubtable trio set a pattern and tradition for the new Museum that obtain to this day. The Museum is not a legacy of ultra-rich patrons. Boston never boasted any Philadelphia Wideners, New York Morgans, or Pittsburgh Mellons. The Museum is rather a legacy of dedicated collectors, working in tandem with wise curators, who built their Museum — Boston's Museum — by their discernment, their desire for physical and intellectual adventure, and their need to follow their own paths and to become Lewis and Clarks in search of new frontiers. The story of the Museum can only be told in such terms. The hazards of this approach within the limits of a foreword are self-evident. As the limited number of objects reproduced in this volume must represent the Museum's great artistic resources, so must an equally arbitrary choice identify the Museum's great human resources in this account of the departments which constitute the Museum of Fine Arts, Boston, for the proud centennial year of 1970.

INTRODUCTION

JAN FONTEIN
Curator, Department of Asiatic Art

The Department of Asiatic Art of the Museum of Fine Arts in Boston has the finest collection of Oriental art under one roof in the world. Thus, although none of the Museum's individual collections can be said to surpass those in the national museums of the parent countries where the works of art originated, it is clear that no other museum in the world in which the arts of India, Southeast Asia, and the Far East are represented together can match the Boston Museum's collection in scope, size, and quality.

Before we proceed to sketch briefly something of the history and background of the farsighted patrons whose efforts have made the Department of Asiatic Art into the unique monument of discerning connoisseurship it is today, it is proper to comment on the circumstances that led to the preeminence of the Museum in the field of Oriental art. There is no question that the extraordinarily high quality of the collection is due in large part to the fact that it was begun at a time when art objects of great artistic merit and importance were still in abundant supply. It is generally taken for granted that this early start was motivated and inspired by the close trading connections between New England and the Far East. The fact that several pioneers to whom we are indebted for our great collections were indeed born in or lived at Salem, Massachusetts, one of the main centers of the China Trade, seems to confirm this supposition. However, upon closer scrutiny of the different factors involved in this process, it would seem that the connection between the China Trade and the presence of such rich collections of Oriental art is less direct than has often been assumed.

To the French, with their traditional attitude of adoration of all things Japanese, Japan was conceived of as a group of beautiful, distant islands, far beyond the horizon, to be admired only from afar. Thus, very few of the chief proponents of *Japonaiserie* in Paris ever set foot in Japan. Consequently their romantic ideas were only rarely representative of the true greatness of Japan and its culture. To the New Englanders, on the other hand, Japan was a tangible geographic reality, a foreign country that could actually be visited if one were inclined to book passage on a merchant ship. As to the China Trade, it had not produced rich collections of Oriental art, for the seclusion in which Chinese art was created and preserved had prevented even those who could have grasped its importance from seeing actual masterpieces. The mariners came back only with what they saw on the waterfront: porcelains for export, paintings on glass, wall paper and gaudy textiles. Nevertheless, the circumstances of the China Trade obviously served to bring the Orient closer to New England. With the growth of interest in Japan, those who were really curious as to what the country was like all considered it perfectly logical to make the voyage and see for themselves. Thus, Bostonians, even if they did not remain totally unaffected by the romantic Parisian vogue, had the opportunity to establish their own criteria of judgment on a more pragmatic basis. Their continuous exposure to the actualities of Japanese life and culture stimulated the development of different, higher standards of collecting, and this resulted, within a very brief span of time, in the growth of great collections of Japanese art. Many of the greatest collectors, motivated by their desire to share their works of art with the public, donated their collections to the new institution that they had helped to found, the Museum of Fine Arts.

The scholars, collectors, and benefactors whose combined efforts resulted in the establishment and development of the Department of Asiatic Art were brought together through a series of coincidences. The first of these men to travel to Japan did not go in search of artistic beauty at all. Edward Sylvester Morse (1838–1925), a Harvard-trained zoologist, set off for Japan in 1877, his objective being to collect specimens of a series of marine fauna known as brachiopods. Morse was among the first foreigners to see the Tōshōgu Shrine at Nikko, now a major tourist attraction, but he hardly paid any attention to it, concentrating instead on the task of collecting shells on the shore of nearby Lake Chūzenji. On the second day after his arrival in Japan he took the train from Yokohama to Tokyo, and from the window he noticed that the recently built railroad cut through a group of large shell mounds. Returning to the spot soon afterwards, he conducted the first archaeological excavation in the history of Japan. The publication of his finds, *Shell Mounds of Omori* (1879), was the first scientific study published by the newly founded University of Tokyo.

Morse was highly systematic as a collector and well versed in the techniques of classifying and cataloguing. When he discovered the infinite variety of contemporary Japanese ceramics, he was fascinated and began to apply all of his great professional skills to assembling a representative collection. The final result of his efforts was an enormous collection numbering well over five thousand pieces. Systematically arranged according to provenance and kilns, they now fill dozens of crowded cases in an attic of the Museum of Fine Arts. Even though the number of pieces of great artistic merit is not large, the collection nevertheless contains a number of well-documented, important archaeological specimens and gives a most thorough and comprehensive view of practically all types of nineteenth-century Japanese pottery.

Much more important, however, than Morse's contributions to the permanent collections of the Museum was his inspiring influence on other Americans whom he persuaded to come to Japan. The first of these was Ernest Francisco Fenollosa (1853–1908), the son of a Spanish-born musician in Salem, Massachusetts, and a neighbor of Morse. He had just finished his studies at Harvard when he received, through Morse's efforts, an appointment as Professor of Philosophy at the University of Tokyo. Fenollosa arrived in Japan one year after Morse, but he was drawn into the orbit of Japanese art much sooner than his mentor had been.

At the time of Fenollosa's arrival in Japan, the prestige of traditional Japanese art had reached a low ebb. It was actually largely due to Fenollosa's energetic efforts that the Japanese gradually came to realize the importance of preserving the relics of their own ancient culture. His important role in the revival of Japanese interest in their own artistic heritage need not be treated here. However, his many activities were not confined to teaching philosophy and propagating a revival of the arts. Another of his projects can best be described in Fenollosa's own words, as he wrote them to Morse: "We have been through all the principal temples in Yamashiro and Yamato armed with government letters and orders, have ransacked godowns, and brought to light pieces of statue from the lowest stratum of debris in the top stories of pagodas 1300 years old. We may say in brief that we have made the first accurate list of the great art treasures kept in the central temples of Japan, we have overturned the traditional criticism attached to these individual specimens for ages. . . ."

The first of these excursions was undertaken in 1880. It seems to have whetted Fenollosa's appetite for collecting, an activity for which he was better qualified than any other Westerner of his time and for which he possessed unusual gifts. The most memorable souvenir of his first trip to Kyoto is the Matsushima screen by Kōrin, now in the Museum of Fine Arts.

In 1882 Fenollosa made his third trip to Japan, accompanied by the Bostonian Dr. William Sturgis Bigelow (1850–1926), who was so fascinated by the country that he stayed on for seven years. He was immediately drawn into Fenollosa's circle and soon started to accompany him on his trips in search of hidden temple treasures. It must have been during one of these early excursions that Bigelow was able to acquire the *Hokkedō Kompon Mandara*, the only painting of the Nara period ever to leave the country. Although Dr. Bigelow became deeply interested in Tendai and Esoteric Buddhism, which he studied with great diligence, he also devoted much of his time to the collecting of Japanese art on a truly grand scale. He had a wide range of interests, and the great variety of important material assembled in his collection is an accurate reflection of the catholicity of his taste.

By the time Bigelow had determined that his collection should go to the Boston Museum, it already consisted of thousands of pieces. But he not only sent his own collection to Boston, he also persuaded his friend Charles Goddard Weld (1857–1911) to buy, in 1886, the entire collection of Ernest Fenollosa, which was sold with the understanding that it was to remain permanently in the Museum of Fine Arts. When it arrived in Boston in 1889, together with the Bigelow collection, and when the two were displayed in the course of the following year, the Museum of Fine Arts had clearly established the preeminence in the field of Japanese art that was henceforth to be a salient characteristic of its collections.

Not long afterwards, Ernest Fenollosa followed the collection that bore his and Dr. Weld's name. In 1890 he was appointed curator of the Japanese Department of the Museum of Fine Arts. The next four years were spent cataloguing and installing the collections and in organizing a series of exhibitions of Japanese art which were undoubtedly the most significant held up to that time.

The last in this series of exhibitions was a traveling show of Lohan paintings from the Daitokuji, Kyoto. These paintings, dating from between 1178 and 1184 and the work of two painters, Chou Chi-ch'ang and Lin T'ing-kuei, are among the finest Chinese Buddhist paintings in existence. Bernard Berenson gave his future wife, Mary Costelloe, an eyewitness report of this exhibition: ". . . To begin with they had composition of figures and groups as perfect and simple as the best we Europeans have ever done. . . . I was prostrate. Fenollosa shivered as he looked, I thought I should die, and even Denman Ross who looked dumpy Anglo-Saxon was jumping up and down. We had to poke and pinch each other's necks and wept. No, decidedly I never had such an art experience." If now, almost seventy-five years after the event, the objects of their highly emotional reactions would fail to meet the fastidious art historical standards of our own times, we still would forgive them. However, that they were deeply moved by creations of the highest artistic order can only increase our admiration for their early understanding and appreciation of Oriental art.

Before the exhibition returned to Japan ten of its paintings ended up in the collection of the Museum of Fine Arts, sold by the Daitokuji to pay for urgently needed temple repairs. It was one of the last contributions that Fenollosa was to make to the collections of the Department of Asiatic Art. Shortly afterwards the circumstances connected with his divorce and remarriage resulted in his leaving the Museum.

With the departure of Ernest Fenollosa the rapid growth of the collections seems to have slowed, only to increase again with the arrival on the Boston scene of one of Fenollosa's Japanese pupils, Okakura Kakuzō (1862–1913). Okakura had accompanied Fenollosa on many of his excursions in search of temple treasures, sharing with him such exciting experiences as the discovery of the Yumedeno Kannon (1884). Afterwards he had headed the new Fine Arts Academy, but in 1898 he separated from this position as well as from his post at the Imperial Museum, Tokyo. It was extremely fortunate for the Museum of Fine Arts that a person of such great talents was available and willing to lead the Department into what was soon to become another era of dynamic expansion.

Okakura Kakuzō was among the greatest connoisseurs of Far Eastern art of his time, equally well versed in Japanese and Chinese art. The importance of many of his acquisitions demonstrates perhaps even more eloquently than his many writings the quality of the man. One of his earliest acquisitions for the Department was a renowned landscape by Bunsei. A colorful personality and a man of many unusual talents, Okakura was able to inspire many others with an interest in Chinese and Japanese art and in the Museum he served. In his successful efforts to expand the collection he was generously assisted by Edward J. Holmes. The greatest contributions that Okakura made to the collections, however, occurred after his death in 1913. Just after he had passed away, Denman Waldo Ross rediscovered in Paris the stone sculpture from the Pai-ma-ssu near Lo-yang, which Okakura had tried in vain to buy in 1906.

Again, some of the greatest works of art in Okakura's private collection, acquired in the years prior to his association with the Boston Museum, had remained preserved at his house in Japan. Seven years after his death these were bought by the Museum. Among these are some of the greatest treasures of the Museum: the Dai-itoku Myō-ō and the Miroku by Kaikei. Another typical example of his refined taste is the beautiful Korean Medicine Buddha.

Okakura was succeeded by John Ellerton Lodge, who became curator in 1915, and who, from 1921 to 1931, held this position concurrently with that of Director of the newly founded Freer Gallery of Art in Washington, D.C. It was during the curatorship of this eminent scholar that the Department, up to that time devoted almost exclusively to the arts of China and Japan, broadened its scope by expanding into the field of Indian and Southeast Asian art. This development was, in large part, because of Denman Waldo Ross, a Cambridge collector who had been a Trustee since 1895 and who had given art objects of high quality to the Museum on various occasions. In 1917, when he made another generous gift to the Museum, he included a large collection of Indian art which had been assembled by Ananda K. Coomaraswamy (1877–1947). Here history repeated itself, for just as Ernest Fenollosa had become curator of his own collection after it had been bought by Dr. Weld, so Ananda Coomaraswamy followed his own

14

collection to Boston after it had been presented to the Museum of Fine Arts by Dr. Ross. Thus, the Museum acquired not only an outstanding collection of Indian art, but also the most brilliant scholar in the field of Indian art of his time. Coomaraswamy remained in Boston for the rest of his life and many of the books of this prolific genius were written here.

As a result of Okakura's vital interest in Chinese art, the Department had begun its collection of Chinese paintings, but it was during the curatorship of Kojiro Tomita, who succeeded Lodge as curator in 1931, that this part of the collection witnessed its greatest expansion. During the thirties many early masterpieces were acquired, including such works as Hui-tsung's *Five-Colored Parakeet* and Yen Li-pên's *The Thirteen Emperors*. After World War II the emphasis shifted to Ming and Ch'ing paintings. The highly successful post-war acquisition program was largely made possible by the very generous bequest of Keith McLeod in 1956.

The curatorship of Kojiro Tomita, whose term of service was one of the longest in the history of the Museum — he joined the staff in 1907 at the age of eighteen and retired as curator in 1962 — was marked by a long succession of brilliant accessions. The scope of the collection was once more expanded in a spectacular way when Charles Bain Hoyt (1889–1949) bequeathed to the Museum his large collection of Oriental art, chiefly of Chinese and Korean ceramics. All types of early Chinese ceramics (with the exception of Chün and Kuan wares) are represented in this collection, each with several choice specimens. As early as World War I Hoyt had become interested in Korean celadons, a field then scorned by most collectors of Oriental ceramics, and it is due to his foresight and munificence that the Museum now has one of the finest collections of Korean ceramics.

By the time my late predecessor, Robert Treat Paine, was appointed Curator of the Department (1962) the possibilities for adding works of art of the quality of those previously acquired had been greatly reduced. It may be said, therefore, that the collection, as it now stands, will probably retain essentially its present form. In a brief survey of the history of the Department such as this, it is impossible to do justice to the numerous benefactors whose generosity has made the Museum of Fine Arts and its Department of Asiatic Art into the great institution that it is. Moreover, other important parts of the collection such as the Japanese print room (which contains more than fifty thousand prints) have not been treated in this book. This necessitates at least a passing reference here to the gift of William S. and John T. Spaulding, whose magnificent prints, often still in prime condition, are only shown to visitors upon request.

Its close ties of long standing with the countries of the Far East and the extraordinary cultural role that some of its curators have performed in the cultural exchange between East and West has given the Department of Asiatic Art its own, unique atmosphere. Year after year scholars from all over the world come to Boston to study the works of art on display and the vast amount of precious material in its storage rooms. Recent years have witnessed the attendance of an increasing number of Japanese visitors, who come to Boston to see the treasures from their homeland — treasures that have, for more than seventy-five years, spread the fame of Oriental art in the New World. It is hoped that this book will make many more decide to come. 15

CHINA

KOREA

JAR WITH COVER. *Chou Dynasty.*

A repeated design of round medallions in square frames has been applied in glass paste on the buff pottery ground. The bright colors of the glass have faded into soft green and gray. Two other pieces of this rare type of late Chou pottery are known to exist: one was in the collection of the late Mrs. Walter Sedgwick, London; the other is in the William Rockhill Nelson Gallery of Art, Kansas City, Missouri.

MONGOLIAN YOUTH. *Chou Period.*

This superb example of early Chinese bronze sculpture shows a young man intently gazing at two birds chained to the top of two sticks he holds vertically in his hands. The figure reveals many details of the dress and hairstyle of the period and is therefore not only a fascinating work of art, but also an important source of evidence for early Chinese cultural history. The figure is said to have been excavated at Chin-ts'un, near Lo-yang (Honan province). Although there is no definite proof of this claim, the figure does seem to fit well into the elegant style of the objects usually associated with this site.

Mongolian Youth
Late Chou period;
circa fourth-third century B.C.
Bronze figure and jade birds; height 11 1/4".
31.976
Maria Antoinette Evans Fund.

Jar with Cover
Late Chou dynasty;
fifth-third century B.C.
Pottery decorated with glass paste
Height 4 1/2", diameter 5 1/2".
50.1841
Charles B. Hoyt Collection.

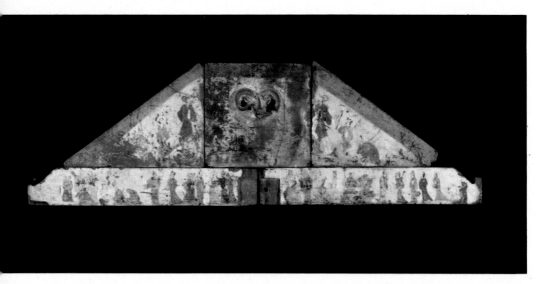

ANIMAL FIGHT IN THE SHANG–LIN PARK. *Han Period.*

This set of tiles, consisting of five pieces, forms a tympanum. It was excavated during World War I from a four-chambered tomb located about two and two-thirds miles west of the present city of Lo-yang (Honan province). The figure scenes painted on it represent men watching fighting animals, presumably the tou-shou (animal fights) staged at the Royal Zoological Park of the Han, in Shang-lin Park. Although parts of the surface had deteriorated before the tiles came to Boston, the excellent draftsmanship of the supple and lively brushwork, together with the delicate coloring, are still clearly visible.

In 1957 Chinese archaeologists excavated a tomb not far from the original location of the Boston tiles. The tympanum discovered in the main burial chamber differs from this piece in that the two triangular sections and the central square slab have a reticulated decoration, but the painted figures on the lower crossbeam are closely related to those on the Boston tiles. The fact that it is decorated on both sides suggests that it was used, like the recently discovered piece, as the tympanum of a partition between the two parts of the main burial chamber, which could be viewed from both sides. As a result of their study comparing architectural features, the excavators date the recently-found tympanum in the late first century B.C. This is considerably earlier than the dates previously suggested for the Boston piece, which range from the second to the fourth century A.D.

BODHISATTVA. *Eastern Wei Period.* p. 22

One of the largest early pieces of stone sculpture ever to come out of China, this finely carved figure shows a close resemblance to the sculptures of the cave-temple complex of Lung-mên, especially to those of cave XXIV, which can be dated by inscription to A.D. 527. The cusped necklace is identical with those of the figures in this cave, but the softly flowing folds of the drapery suggest a slightly later date, possibly in the early years of the East-

Bodhisattva
Early Eastern Wei period; circa A.D. 530
Gray limestone, yellowed by burial;
height 6'6''.
13.2804
Gift of Denman Waldo Ross in memory
of Okakura Kakuzō.

22

ern Wei period. The details of the back are partially carved, an indication that the figure was not originally part of a cave temple.

In the spring of 1903, while visiting the temple Pai-ma-ssŭ near Lo-yang, the Japanese painter and amateur archaeologist Hayasaki Kōkichi saw a group of Chinese excavate this statue from the central courtyard of the temple. Although he and Okakura Kakuzō repeatedly tried to acquire it, the sculpture disappeared from the temple, to reappear in Paris shortly before Okakura's death.

Attributed to YEN LI–PÊN. *The Thirteen Emperors.*
The scroll consists of a series of thirteen portraits of emperors and their attendants. The criteria used in making this selection are unclear, for the personages do not seem to have been chosen for their historical importance. The earliest is an emperor of the former Han dynasty, the last is the second and last emperor of the Sui dynasty. The first six portraits (the emperors are not represented in their exact chronological order) are obviously copies, made to reproduce a missing section of the scroll. This section probably dates from the Northern Sung period. The last seven paintings, however,

YEN LI-PÊN (?)
Died 673
The Thirteen Emperors
Detail.
T'ang period; seventh century A.D.
Handscroll, ink and colors on silk
Height 20 1/4", length 17 1/2".
31.643
Denman Waldo Ross Collection.

are of a much earlier date, possibly from the seventh century. This was the period when the celebrated court painter Yen Li-pên was active, and — as early as Northern Sung times — the scroll was attributed to this master. There is nothing in the style of painting that would contradict this early attribution. On the contrary, the lack of a background, the sensitive brushwork, the soft coloring, and the decorative shading all indicate an early date and make this handscroll one of the great masterpieces of early Chinese figure painting.

CH'ÊN YUNG–CHIH. *Buddha Under the Mango Tree.*

This painting represents a miracle which the Buddha performed as a preliminary to the Great Miracle of Srāvastī. At the command of the Buddha the gardener Ganda planted a mango seed, whereupon a mango tree sprang up immediately. Almost instantly it was covered with flowers and fruit. The Buddha, who holds a mango in his hand, is dressed in a red robe which is drawn in closely spaced, undulating lines of ink and gold. The luxuriant tree winds upward in powerful curves. The pigments in which the rocks, trees, leaves, and fruit are rendered have been piled up so as to create a low relief. The style of the drapery and this unusual relief technique have both been traditionally associated with the seventh-century Central Asian painter Yü-ch'ih I-sêng. The painting was attributed to this celebrated master until recently, when a signature was discovered in the lower left corner reading: "respectfully copied by Ch'ên Yung-chih." It is probable that Ch'ên Yung-chih, an early eleventh-century court artist, copied the painting from a work of Yü-ch'ih I-sêng, possibly one from the imperial collection. Numerous seals allow us to trace the painting's history to Sung Hui-tsung and the collection of Yang Shih (1053–1135). Recently a thick coat of brown glue was removed, revealing for the first time the brilliance of the original colors.

CH'ÊN YUNG-CHIH
Buddha Under the Mango Tree
Sung period; circa 1025
Ink and colors on paper; 7' × 28".
56.256
Keith McLeod Fund.

Right: detail.

On pages 26–27:
EMPEROR HUI-TSUNG
1082–1135
Ladies Preparing Newly Woven Silk
Detail.
Sung period; early twelfth century
Handscroll, ink and colors on silk
Height 14 1/2", length 57 1/4".
12.886
Chinese and Japanese Special Fund.

EMPEROR HUI–TSUNG. *Ladies Preparing Newly Woven Silk.*

pp. 26–27

This handscroll by Hui-tsung is the result of a combination of two of the Emperor's interests: painting and collecting. Although unsigned, the painting carries an inscription by Chang-tsung (reigned 1188–1208) of the Chin dynasty, attributing the painting to Hui-tsung and calling it a copy of an earlier painting by the T'ang artist Chang Hsüan (early eighth century), which was in Hui-tsung's vast collection. Although Chang-tsung is not known as an authoritative connoisseur of Chinese painting, he was nevertheless distantly related to Hui-tsung, and may therefore have been in a good position to judge the authenticity of the painting.

The original painting by Chang Hsüan has been lost and we have no way of judging how scrupulously Hui-tsung copied it. Like Yen Li-pên's *Emperors,*

the ladies — dressed like some of the T'ang tomb figurines — stand in empty space. In a dignified manner they go about their tasks of pounding the silk and drawing out the thread. The unusually bright colors of the scroll may represent the preservation of one of the stylistic traditions of T'ang period painting.

EMPEROR HUI–TSUNG. *The Five-Colored Parakeet.*

Among the treasures of the Department of Asiatic Art are the two paintings by the Emperor-painter Hui-tsung of the Sung dynasty, a gifted artist whose tragic life ended while he was held in captivity by the Jurčen tribe in Manchuria. This painting dates from the time he was still his own master. It represents a five-colored parakeet which the Emperor discovered in his palace

EMPEROR HUI-TSUNG
The Five-Colored Parakeet
Sung period; early twelfth century
Handscroll, ink and colors on silk
Height 21″, length 49 1/4″.
The painting was once in the collection of the Mongol Emperor Wên-tsung (reigned 1329–1332).
33.364
Maria Antoinette Evans Fund.

28

garden. In order to commemorate this event, he painted a sensitive and accurate likeness of the exotic bird and composed a poem, which is written in his elegant hand. The painting carries the seal and a partly obliterated signature of the artist. Although there is considerable uncertainty as to which of several extant paintings of birds were actually painted by Hui-tsung, this painting is undoubtedly one of the finest of this type and was most likely executed by the imperial artist himself.

KUAN–YIN. *Sung Period.*

The compassionate Bodhisattva Kuan-yin (Sanskrit: Avalokiteśvara) is represented in the posture of Royal Relaxation (Sanskrit: Mahārājalīla), the right arm supported by the raised right knee, the left leg hanging down and

Kuan-yin
Sung period; circa twelfth century
Polychromed wood; height 55 1/2".
20.590
Harvey Edward Wetzel Fund.

29

the head slightly inclined. During the Sung and Chin dynasties, this type of wooden sculpture was common in northern China, especially in Shansi province. During the restoration a thick layer of later overpainting was removed from the image, revealing bright colors as well as kirigane designs (cut gold foil) underneath. As a result, the original resplendent quality of the figure is now apparent. Images of this type were commonly placed in front of brightly colored wall-paintings representing the legendary abode of Avalokiteśvara at Potalaka.

Traditionally attributed to TUNG YÜAN. *Clear Weather in the Valley.* This masterpiece of early Chinese landscape painting has for many centuries been attributed to the tenth-century master Tung Yüan. Although we have little first-hand knowledge of the stylistic characteristics of Tung Yüan's work, the present handscroll would seem to breathe a spirit which is quite different from that of the few surviving tenth-century landscapes. Painted with a superb feeling for atmospheric perspective, it reveals a poetic sentiment which is typical of the landscape masters of the Southern Sung period.

CHOU CHI–CH'ANG. *Arhats Bestowing Alms Upon Beggars.*
This painting, together with nine others in the collection, was originally part of a set of one hundred paintings showing the Five Hundred Arhats. The set belongs to the Daitokuji in Kyoto. Forty-four of these were exhibited in

30

TUNG YÜAN (?)
907–960
Clear Weather in the Valley
Sung period; twelfth-thirteenth century
Handscroll, ink and slight colors on paper;
14 3/4″ × 59 1/2″.
12.903
Chinese and Japanese Special Fund.

CHOU CHI-CH'ANG
Arhats Bestowing Alms Upon Beggars
Sung period; dated 1184
Ink and colors on silk; 44" × 21".
95.4
General Fund.

31

the United States in a traveling exhibition, organized by Ernest Fenollosa, in 1894. At the close of the exhibition the Museum of Fine Arts acquired ten of these paintings, while two additional paintings, not included in that exhibition, were sold to Charles L. Freer and are now in the Freer Gallery of Art, Washington, D.C. The temple still possesses eighty-two paintings.

Some of the paintings of this set bear dedicatory inscriptions in gold which indicate that the set was made between 1178 and 1184 for the temple Hui-an-yüan, near Ning-po (Chêkiang province). Some of them are signed by Chou Chi-ch'ang, others by Lin T'ing-kuei, both of whom were probably professional painters. Taken to Japan during the thirteenth century, the set played an important role in the iconographical evolution of Japanese paintings of Arhats. The entire set was copied by the famous monk-painter Minchō (1352–1431) in 1386 and is now in the Tōfukuji, Kyoto.

CH'ÊN JUNG. *The Nine Dragons.*
In an extraordinary display of powerful and versatile brushwork the artist has painted nine dragons of different types and in varying poses, gamboling among clouds and waves. Ch'ên Jung, who was famous for this genre, added two inscriptions, from one of which we learn that he painted this scroll in the year 1244. Among several similar works attributed to Ch'ên Jung —

32

CH'ÊN JUNG
Flourished 1210–1260
The Nine Dragons
Detail.
Sung period; dated 1244
Handscroll, ink with touches of red on paper
Height 18 1/4", length 36'.
17.1697
Francis Gardner Curtis Fund.

including part of another scroll also in the Museum of Fine Arts — this painting stands out as a superb example of his great talent.

WINE BOTTLE. *Northern Sung Period.*

The pearl-punched ground for the incised decoration, which has been filled in with a reddish brown color, is typical of the products of the kilns of Ch'ü-ho in Têng-fêng-hsien (Honan province), an important center for the production of Ta'ŭ-chou-type wares during the Sung period. Around the short neck is a floral design, and on the central band of the vase are three figures carrying gourds on sticks over their shoulders.

Wine Bottle
Northern Sung period;
eleventh-twelfth century
Tz' ŭ-chou type
Height 15 1/2″, diameter 7 3/4″.
50.1058
Charles B. Hoyt Collection.

VASE. *Korea, Koryŏ Period.*

The vase is decorated with a simple design of cranes and bamboo, which has been incised into the surface of the paste and then filled in with white and greenish black slip. The vase was then covered with the celadon-green glaze. Throughout their history, the Koreans had a strong predilection for inlaid decoration and they applied this technique in their metalwork, their lacquers, and their ceramics. The simplicity of the design indicates that this vase is one of the relatively early examples of inlaid celadon, made not long after this technique was first developed and perfected.

Vase (*Maebyŏng*)
Korea, Koryŏ period; twelfth century
Celadon, inlaid decoration
Height 12 1/2″, diameter 7″.
50.989
Charles B. Hoyt Collection.

JAPAN

DAI–ITOKU MYŌ–Ō. *Heian Period.*

This dramatic rendering of the six-armed, six-legged Dai-itoku Myō-ō (Sanskrit: Yamāntaka) shows this important figure of the Esoteric Buddhist pantheon in all his awesome power and glory. The contrast of the strong, bold outlines with the delicate details of the attributes and cloth patterns, the bright, sparkling colors, and the lively rendering of the flames surrounding the seated figure are typical of Japanese Buddhist painting of the eleventh century.

This masterpiece, perhaps the finest Buddhist painting ever to leave Japan, is one of the great discoveries of Okakura Kakuzō, who acquired it just before he resigned in 1898 as a curator of the Imperial Museum, Tokyo. During all the years of Okakura's travels and his stay in Boston, it remained in storage in his house in Japan, to be exhibited only once in the Kyoto Museum shortly after his death. Four years after the Memorial Exhibition in 1916 it was acquired by the Museum of Fine Arts. There are very few paintings of this size and importance of which the original provenance cannot be established; however, as the story of its provenance from the Daigoji in Kyoto has been disproved, the ultimate origin of this Dai-itoku Myō-ō remains shrouded in mystery.

GIGAKU MASK. *Heian Period.* *p. 38*

This finely carved mask is an outstanding example of early Japanese woodcarving. Originally it must have been painted in bright colors and fitted with heavy eyebrows and a beard. The animated expression of the face with its protruding tongue is very similar to that of the so-called *Ni no mai* masks of the Bugaku dancers. As is the case with the *Ni no mai* masks, the specific context in which this mask was used is not clear.

In the illustrated catalogue *Shūko Jūshū* which appeared in 1800, Matsudaira Sadanobu (1758–1829) published drawings of thirty-eight Gigaku masks in the collection of the Tōdaiji temple in Nara. Of these masks, nineteen are still in the temple's collection. One of the drawings shows a mask that is almost identical in shape and size to the Boston piece, and the indi-

Dai-itoku Myō-ō
Heian period; late eleventh century
Ink, colors and kirigane on silk;
6'3 1/2" × 46 1/2".
20.750
Gift of William Sturgis Bigelow in
memory of Okakura Kakuzō.

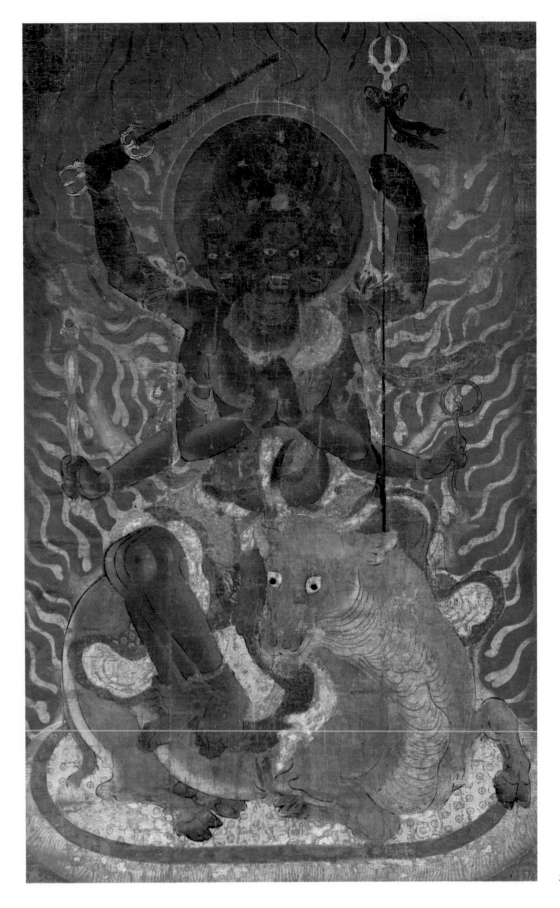

Gigaku Mask
Heian period; circa eleventh century
Polychromed wood; height 10 1/2".
11.5940
William Sturgis Bigelow Collection.

cations of color given on the drawing correspond to the faded colors on the mask. In all likelihood the two pieces are identical.

DAI–ITOKU MYŌ–Ō. *Heian Period.*

This refined, superbly conceived image of Dai-itoku Myō-ō has lost little of its original artistic impact, even though it is now in a rather fragmentary state. The top of the knot of hair on the head has been partially restored. Although it is not known whether the remarkably well-preserved colors are original, it is unlikely that they are later than the Kamakura period. The statue represents a transitional stage from the one-block (*ichiboku*) technique to the joint-block (*yosegi*) technique. It conveys the Heian period's new and more humane approach to Esoteric Buddhism.

38

Dai-itoku Myō-ō
Heian period; tenth-eleventh century
Painted wood; height 36 1/2".
05.228
Special Japanese Fund.

Dainichi As Ichijikinrin
Heian period; late twelfth century
Ink and colors on silk; 49 1/4″ × 31 1/4″.
09.387
Gift of Denman Waldo Ross.

KAIKEI
Miroku Bosatsu
Kamakura period; A.D. 1189
Wood, partially covered with
gold lacquer; height 42″.
20.723
Chinese and Japanese Special Fund.

DAINICHI AS ICHIJIKINRIN. *Heian Period.*   *p. 40*

Nyo-irin Kannon
Early Kamakura period; circa 1200
Ink, colors and gold on silk;
38 3/4" × 17 3/4".
11.4032
Fenollosa-Weld Collection.

Right: detail.

Dainichi as Ichijikinrin (Sanskrit: Ekākṣara-uṣnīṣacakra) is seated cross-legged in the "diamond pose" on a white lotus, forming with his hands the *chiken-in* or "wisdom fist." Flanked by four flower vases and with the Five Buddhas in his headdress, this representation of Mahāvairocana as the Lord of the Vajradhātu is in strict accordance with the iconographic regulations for Vajradhātu mandalas. Several closely related paintings of this type exist, including another slightly later example also in the Museum of Fine Arts.

The painting, partly colored from the back (*urasaishiki*), has lost some of its original coloring and several details have become blurred. A notice of its repair and remounting, dating from 1907, is signed by the abbot of the Jingoji monastery near Kyoto. Shortly after, it was sold to Dr. Ross, who presented it to the Museum.

KAIKEI. *Miroku Bosatsu.*   *p. 41*

This superb specimen of twelfth-century Japanese sculpture in joint-block (*yosegi*) technique originally came from the Kōfukuji at Nara. It represents the Bodhisattva Miroku (Sanskrit: Maitreya), the Buddha of the Future. It was given to Okakura Kakuzō in 1903–4. Five years later, when the statue had to be repaired because its head had become loose, a sūtra scroll was discovered inside. A colophon added to this scroll mentions the date of Bunji 5th year (A.D. 1189) and the name of the sculptor Kaikei. It is the earliest known dated work by this celebrated Buddhist monk-sculptor. This sculpture and the painting representing Dai-itoku Myō-ō (see page 37), both from the collection of Okakura Kakuzō, are among the greatest masterpieces of Japanese Buddhist art in the Museum.

NYO–IRIN KANNON. *Kamakura Period.*

The six-armed Nyo-irin Kannon (Sanskrit: Cintāmaṇicakra) is represented in the attitude of "royal ease" on Mount Potalaka, the legendary abode of Avalokiteśvara which is known for its many waterfalls. Although the richly adorned golden figure is painted in strict accordance with the iconographic rules, the addition of three attendants in the lower left corner is somewhat unusual. Basu Sennin (Sanskrit: Rṣi Vasu), Kichijōten (Sanskrit: Mahāśrī), and Zennishi Dōji (Sanskrit: Janavasabha), are more often associated with the Thousand-armed Avalokiteśvara and Vaiśravaṇa than with Cintāmaṇicakra.

The date of this painting is disputed by scholars, some assigning it to the late Heian period, others attributing it to the early Kamakura period. Stylistic affinities with works dating from about 1200 suggest a date in that period. It is probably slightly earlier than a similar painting in the Freer Gallery of Art, Washington, D.C.

KIBI DAIJIN NITTŌ E–KOTOBA. *Heian Period.*

This famous handscroll illustrates the legendary adventure of the ambassador to the Chinese court, Kibi no Makibi, during his mission to T'ang China in 753. Aided by the ghost of the celebrated poet Abe no Nakamaro, the skillful magician Kibi successfully passes the rigorous tests of skill and learning to which he is subjected by his haughty Chinese hosts. The purely fictional story — Abe no Nakamaro was still alive at the time of Kibi's mission — seems to be of the *engi* type. In it the descendants of Kibi no Makibi saw a support for their claim of supremacy over the descendants of Abe no Nakamaro in the field of On'yōdō, a generic term for various magical and pseudo-scientific practices of Chinese origin. During the Heian period both families regarded these practices as their specialty.

Executed in bright colors with great skill and an exquisite sense of humor, this scroll, recently divided into four parts in order to ensure its preservation, is one of the finest examples of Yamato-e painting in the United States. Its removal from Japan resulted in the first Japanese legislation making the export of art objects subject to governmental approval.

Kibi Daijin Nittō E-kotoba
Detail.
Heian period; late twelfth century
Ink and colors on paper
Handscroll; height 12 3/4", length 80'.
32.131
William Sturgis Bigelow collection
by exchange.

KŌSHUN
Sōgyō Hachiman
Kamakura period; A.D. 1328
Wood, crystal eyes; height 32 1/4".
36.413
Maria Antoinette Evans Fund
and contribution.

Bishamonten Mandara
Kamakura period; early thirteenth century
Ink, colors and gold on silk;
47″ × 26 3/4″.
Acquired for the Museum by Okakura
Kakuzō, it is said to have come from
the Enryakuji on Mt. Hieizan.
05.202
Chinese and Japanese Special Fund.

KŌSHUN. *Sōgyō Hachiman.* *p. 45*

Sōgyō Hachiman, the Shintō deity Hachiman in the guise of a Buddhist priest, is a figure associated with syncretic Shintō, a religious development in which Japan's native Shintō gods came to be regarded as manifestations of figures from the Buddhist pantheon. This fine sculpture, executed in the joint-block (*yosegi*) technique, carries an inscription inside the head. The inscription indicates that the sculpture was carved by Kōshun, a monk-sculptor of the rank of Hōgen, at the Kōfukuji, Nara. About his life little is known, but dated sculptures by this master range from A.D. 1311 to 1369. Although there is an error in the name of the era mentioned in the inscription, the statue must have been carved in the third year of Kareki, i.e. A.D. 1328.

BISHAMONTEN MANDARA. *Kamakura Period.*

Of all existing representations of Bishamonten (Sanskrit: Vaiśravana) this mandala is one of the most complex, combining iconographic features of different types of representations of Bishamonten into one lively and colorful scene. It is only in the compendium of iconographic drawings by Shingaku (1117–80), the famous *Besson zakki* (no. 289), that we find the Guardian King of the North surrounded by a larger retinue. Supported by the triad made up of the Earth Goddess, Niramba and Biramba, Vaiśravana stands surrounded by his relatives and attendants. To his right we see Kichijōten and Zennishi dōji. The four-armed figure in the background can be identified as Karuratenshi, a rare figure of minor importance in the Buddhist pantheon, who also appears in iconographic drawings as an attendant of Vaiśravana. Five Yaksas stand to the left of Bishamonten; they are accompanied by two Rāksasas in the foreground.

The artist, a superbly skilled draftsman, has rendered the profusion of iconographic details in a most meticulous and orderly, yet also imaginative and lively way. Although attributed by some to the late Heian period, from a stylistic point of view this masterpiece of Japanese Buddhist painting would seem to fit best among the works of the early Kamakura period.

HEIJI MONOGATARI EMAKI. *Kamakura Period.* *pp. 48–51*

The wars between the Taira and Minamoto clans were an episode in the eventful history of feudal Japan which remained, through the ages, an inexhaustible source of inspiration for artists. The earliest extant pictorial rendering of these events, and one of the most impressive, is a series of handscrolls known as the Heiji Monogatari Emaki. Once a large series of handscrolls, it now consists of only three scrolls and some scattered fragments. The scroll reproduced here is the finest of the three. The anonymous artist has illustrated the night attack on Sanjō Palace in 1159 by the combined forces of Fujiwara Nobuyori and Minamoto Yoshitomo, and the subsequent abduction of the retired Emperor Go-Shirakawa. The painting represents the culmination of a technique for which the Yamato-e artists were famous:

the skillful handling of large crowds of people. The artist has done justice to the individuality of each person; yet at the same time he has managed to convey the nervous tension of the battlefield by creating, out of the countless individual persons, crowds that have an organic unity of their own, moving towards the scene of the battle and regrouping afterwards around the imperial carriage. Between these two crowds lies the Palace, going up in flames, while the scene dissolves into scattered hand-to-hand fights, full of the fierce brutality that characterized these civil wars.

Heiji Monogatari Emaki
(*The Burning of the Sanjō Palace*)
Left and below: details.
Kamakura period; late thirteenth century
Ink and colors on paper
Handscroll; height 16 1/4″,

length 22′11 1/2″.
Acquired by Mr. Fenollosa before 1886.
11.4000
Fenollosa-Weld Collection.

On pages 50–51: detail.

Above:
Dish
Edo period; late seventeenth century
Ko-Kutani porcelain; diameter 13 3/4".
34.78
Edward S. Morse Memorial Fund.

Above, right:
Jar
Edo period; late seventeenth century
Kakiëmon porcelain, enamelled decoration;
height 8", diameter 6 1/2".
57.383
Edward S. Morse Memorial Fund.

Vase
Kamakura period; fourteenth century
Pottery, yellowish glaze;
height 10", diameter 7".
19.880
Gift of Miss Theodora Lyman.

VASE. *Kamakura Period.*

This vase is a fine example of Ko-Seto ware of the Kamakura period. The impressed design of chrysanthemum scrolls is covered with a thin, crackled yellowish glaze. This vase was given to the Museum on loan in 1915; at that time it was described as a Chinese piece.

DISH. *Edo Period.*

The dish is decorated with a landscape within an octagonal double frame, surrounded by eight medallions against a background of swastika patterns. The decoration is executed in green, yellow, blue, red, black, and aubergine enamels, a color scheme that is typical of the early products of the Kutani kilns.

JAR. *Edo Period.*

This porcelain jar with a flat shoulder, short neck and wide mouth is decorated with chrysanthemums and rocks in red, yellow, blue, and green enamels. The vertical zigzag design on the neck and the petal rays around the shoulder are often found on the wares of the early Kakiëmon potters. A dull, cream-colored crackled ground occurs on several other pieces of this type. It is generally attributed to one of the first three Kakiëmon masters, but the identification of their wares is still largely a matter of speculation.

53

THE GAY QUARTERS OF KYOTO. *Edo Period.*

In the manner characteristic of the genre painters of the second half of the seventeenth century, the anonymous artist has painted a vivid impression of the colorful life in the gay quarters of Kyoto. One screen (06.286) shows a crowd of people strolling along a street lined with houses of pleasure. The other screen (illustrated here) shows a large tea house with a garden full of people amusing themselves. The two outside panels of this last screen were lost and have been replaced by panels that carry specimens of the handwriting of the priest Takasubu Ryūtatsu. The first of the forty-six poems, in the upper right corner, is the Kimigayo, here written in exactly the same version as that of the present national anthem of Japan. In the lower left corner, the last of the eight sheets carries the signature of Ryūtatsu and a date corresponding to 1602.

THEATERS ALONG SHIJŌ STREET. *Edo Period.*   pp. 56–57

On two six-fold screens, the artist has given a panoramic view of the Shijō Kawaramachi section in Kyoto, extending as far as the Kamo River. This was the theater district of the ancient capital, and the streets are lined with theaters of many different types. The accurate and lively rendering of innumerable details makes this pair of screens a fascinating document for our knowledge of mid-seventeenth century Japanese theater.

On pages 56–57:
Theaters Along Shijō Street
Detail.
Edo period; circa mid-seventeenth
century
Ink, colors, and gold on paper
Pair of six-fold screens;
each panel 41″ × 19 1/2″.
11.4591–4592

The Gay Quarters of Kyoto
Edo period; second half of the
seventeenth century
Ink, colors, and gold on paper
Pair of six-fold screens;
each panel 41″ × 18″.
06.286–287
Gift of Denman Waldo Ross.

Right: detail.

THE ARRIVAL OF A PORTUGUESE SHIP IN JAPAN. *Edo Period.*

This screen is one of a well-known genre in which Japanese artists of the
Kano school, following the vogue of the day, illustrated the arrival of the
"Southern Barbarians" (Namban) in Japan. The left side of this screen is
taken up entirely by a fanciful rendering of a Portuguese carrack; from it,
merchandise is being unloaded into a sloop. From the shore (not shown
here) the "kapitan" watches the proceedings, escorted by a servant holding a payoong over his master's head; meanwhile, the Japanese shopkeepers
in the background await the disembarkation. The foreigners' faces have been
reduced to a uniform stereotype. Thus, there is little distinction between the
Portuguese and the Indian servants with their dark complexions. The other
screen of this pair represents a view of a Chinese harbor, a rather unusual
theme in this genre.

THEATER SCENES AT FUKIYA–CHŌ. *Edo Period.*

This double-faced screen shows, on one side, an interior theater scene, with
a large group of actors on stage and spectators. The entire scene is framed
in clouds of gold. The reverse side shows the entrances to a row of theaters

*The Arrival of a
Portuguese Ship in Japan*
Detail.
Edo period; early seventeenth century
Ink, colors, and gold on paper
Six-fold screen;
each panel 60 3/4″ × 23 1/2″.
11.4168
Fenollosa-Weld Collection

along the Fukiya-chō in the theater district of Edo. A logical connection between the two sides is established; for the theater to the right on the reverse panel is that represented by the interior view.

The artist has rendered the two scenes with painstaking attention to such details as the texts of the theater bills (*bangumi*) and the costumes of the actors. Of special interest is the view (shown here) of the interior of the *jōruri* theater, the Isenodaijō, which appears on the left, above the roof line of the theaters. Although Wakatsuki has tried to establish 1674 or 1675 as the date of the painting on the basis of the posted programs of the theaters, the style of painting suggests a date of at least twenty-five years later.

Theater Scenes at Fukiya-chō
Detail.
Edo period; late seventeenth-
early eighteenth century
Ink, colors, and gold on paper
Six-fold screens; each panel
21 1/4″ × 11 1/4″.
11.4623
Fenollosa-Weld Collection.

59

OGATA KŌRIN. *Matsushima.*

In this grandiose composition, obviously inspired by Sōtatsu's earlier rendering of the same theme (Freer Gallery of Art, Washington, D.C.), Kōrin has skillfully symbolized the scenery of the archipelago in the bay of Matsushima northeast of Sendai. The almost eight hundred islands constitute one of the three Famous Views of Japan. The pine-clad rocks of Matsushima rising from the foam-shaped waves were an ideal theme for the masters of the Rimpa school, who repeated it again and again in their works. The fact that Kōrin signs his name as Hokkyō, an honorary title he received when he was forty-four years old, suggests that this screen, probably one of a pair, was painted after the turn of the century. This screen is one of the first purchases of Ernest Fenollosa, made on his first trip to Kyoto in 1880. It is, in all probability, the first major work of Japanese art to be acquired by a foreigner.

TORII KIYONAGA. *A Mother and Daughter Under a Willow Tree.*
The daughter, who is sitting on a bench, turns toward her mother who is standing next to her. The mother is dressed in a *kasuri* kimono, the daughter in a pale beige kimono. The mother-and-daughter theme occurs frequently in Kiyonaga's work. Between 1782 and 1787 Kiyonaga started to use his original family name Seki again, as an indication of his wish to make himself independent of the Torii traditions and to establish his own artistic style. This painting is an example of his style of around 1785, and is signed Seki Kiyonaga.

OGATA KŌRIN
1658–1716
Matsushima
Edo period; early eighteenth century
Ink and colors on paper
Six-fold screen;
each panel 61″ × 24 3/4″.
11.4584
Fenollosa-Weld Collection.

60

TORII KIYONAGA
1752–1815
*A Mother and Daughter Under
a Willow Tree*
Edo period; late eighteenth century
Ink and colors on silk;
34 1/2″ × 13 3/4″.
11.7531
William Sturgis Bigelow Collection.

SPRING AND AUTUMN FLOWERS. *Edo Period.*

Whereas most sliding doors that have come out of Japan have been re-mounted as folding screens, these panels have retained their original shape, frames, and metal fittings. They are typical representatives of a more ostentatious trend in decoration which developed during the eighteenth century and which gradually replaced the subdued and subtle effects of the decorative styles of the preceding century. The delineation of shapes is somewhat sharper and the color scheme is more varied and harder than that of the earlier works of the Kōrin Kōetsu tradition, to which these panels are obviously related. The panels bear no signature, and it is difficult to attribute them to any specific master in the Kōrin school. There is a certain resemblance to the works of Sakai Hōitsu (1761–1828), who often painted in the manner of Kōrin during his later years when he lived in Kyoto. The panels may have been painted by one of the painters from his atelier.

Spring and Autumn Flowers
Edo period; early eighteenth century
Ink, colors, gold, and silver on paper
Set of four fusuma-panels;
each 66 1/4″ × 27 1/4″.
17.805–808
Denman Waldo Ross Collection.

INDIA
CAMBODIA
NEPAL
IRAN
IRAQ

YAKSĪ.

This torso of a tree-dryad (yaksī) originally served as a bracket figure on one of the gateways (torana), probably the south, of the great Buddhist stūpa at Sanchi. During the first century B.C., Buddhist artists enriched their repertoire by incorporating themes and motifs prevalent in secular as well as religious life. Technically, this torso exemplifies the artist's complete understanding of the structural elements of the female form and its sculptural possibilities. The peculiarly Indian artistic approach to the human form — to envision it as abstraction without, however, distilling its sensuous grace — is already apparent in this elegant lady. Carved fully in the round, the modelling is confined to the essential planes; yet the figure conveys a feeling for naturalism and sensuousness seldom surpassed by later Indian sculptors. The ample breasts, the luxuriant hips and the prominent pelvis symbolize her function as a fertility spirit. The treatment of the long tresses on the back, falling down to the hip, is as simple and effective as the girdle that accentuates her nudity.

GAUTAMA BUDDHA. *p. 66*

The figure is a classic example in metal of the Buddha-image in the mature Gupta style. With assured elegance, the left hand gathers the end of the robe, leaving the right shoulder and arm bare and free. All the auspicious signs of greatness such as the curly hair, the cranial bump, the extended earlobes, etc. are fully developed. The bronze is probably from Buddhapad near Bezwada, an area in which Buddhism was still quite prevalent during the sixth century. The shape of the face, the modelling and proportions of the figure, the graceful *déhanchement,* the half-cast eyes, and full lips, however, clearly reflect the pervading influence of the Sarnath school. Such images, in turn, were responsible for the spread of Indian styles to other South Asian countries.

DURGĀ AS THE SLAYER OF THE BUFFALO DEMON. *p. 66*

The eight-armed goddess stands triumphant in graceful *tribhanga* on the head of the buffalo demon whom she has destroyed. Among the recognizable symbols are the trident, the sword, the discus and the arrow in the right hands, and the shield, the conch, and the bow in the left. In her emanation as Mahisāsuramarddinī, Durgā is worshipped in India as the symbol of "primordial energy," triumphing over evil, personified by the demon. A superb example of the mature and sophisticated Pallava style of the late seventh century, this statue is closely related to the Mamallapuram monuments. The Pallava artists developed a sophisticated artistic idiom of their own, which continued the earlier Andhra manner of slim and elegantly proportioned figures, combined with a dynamic vitality that is probably inspired by the Hindu themes.

THE BODHISATTVA'S BATH IN THE NIRAÑJANĀ RIVER.
p. 67

This fragment was originally part of an enclosing wall. The scene shows the bath of the Bodhisattva, Siddhārtha — who is represented symbolically

64

Yaksī
India, Sanchi; circa 25 B.C.
Height 28 1/4".
29.999
Ross Collection.

by footprints — in the Nirañjanā River. Indra is shown bowing before the footprints; on the other side are the nāga king Kālika, who had predicted the Bodhisattva's future enlightenment, and his two wives. Above are the four river-goddesses, each bearing a vase of plenty. The composition is typical of early Buddhist narrative art, the figures being arranged schematically in rows. By emphasizing the diagonal in the disposition of the arms and legs of the females in the upper register, however, the artist has animated the composition, although the emphasis, as in all such works, is on direct visual communication.

Durgā as the Slayer of the Buffalo Demon
India, Pallava; seventh century A.D.
Dark granulite; height 59″.
27.171
Ross Collection.

Gautama Buddha
India, Bezwada (?); sixth century A.D.
Bronze; height 19 3/4″.
21.1504
Gift of the Government Museum, Madras.

The Bodhisattva's Bath in the Nirañjanā River
Detail.
India, Amaravati; first century A.D.
Greenish limestone;
height 63″, width 39 1/2″,
diameter 5 3/4″.
29.151
Ross Collection.

Dancing Apsaras
Cambodia; eleventh century
Bronze; height 15 1/2".
22.686
Ross Collection.

DANCING APSARAS.

The elegant apsaras is shown dancing on a lotus that springs from the stem of a flowering spray. The spray terminates in a half-open bud, revealing a similar but hieratic female figure, holding a flower in each hand. The dancer's hands touch a flame-fringed trifoliate arch that springs from dragon bases. She is elaborately ornamented and crowned, although the torso is bare. A remarkably alive and animated bronze, it expresses the sinuous and lyrical qualities of the Khmer style.

AMITĀBHA WITH ACOLYTES.

The crowned figure in the center is one of the Tathāgata Amitābha. He is

Amitābha with Acolytes
Nepal; twelfth-thirteenth century
Gouache on cloth; 16 1/4" × 13".
67.818
Gift of John Goelet.

flanked by the Bodhisattvas, Maitreya and Avalokitelśvara, while six other
figures are seated on either side of his head. Other Tathāgatas and divinities
of the Vajrayāna pantheon are represented along the top and bottom. The
painting seems to represent the mandala of the eight great Bodhisattvas, the
earliest representation of which is to be found in Ellora. The concept of the
eight Bodhisattvas seems to have gained popularity in Central Asia, Nepal
and Tibet at this period. One of the earliest known Nepali paintings, this
work is stylistically closely related to illuminations in eleventh and twelfth
century dated manuscripts. Although the composition is determined by the
iconography, both in the refinement of the drawing and in the soft tonality
of the colors, it is a masterpiece of Nepali painting.

HAWK ATTACKING A DUCK.

This stucco relief, presumably used as a wall decoration, was discovered
during the Persian expedition at Rayy (six miles southeast of Teheran) in

Hawk Attacking a Duck
Persia (Iran), Rayy;
tenth-eleventh century
Stucco; height 12 1/4".
35.915
University Museum — Museum of
Fine Arts Persian expedition.

the Buwaihid-Seljug layer. It represents a hawk pouncing upon a duck. The birds are rendered conceptually, but the artist displays acute observation of life in his treatment of the hawk pecking the neck of the unfortunate duck. At the same time, the entire composition reflects a great sense of design by the way the outlines of the two birds flow into each other. The symbolism of such motifs in an Islamic context is still undetermined, but it seems to have been a popular motif in the Mediterranean world, for it frequently occurs in Byzantine art as far west as Greece.

BOWL.

Bowl
Persia (Iran), late twelfth-
early thirteenth century
Minai ware.
Pottery; height 3 1/4″, diameter 8″.
63.1391
Gift of Miss Helen Norton in
memory of Harry A. Norton.

The main part of the bowl is occupied by a king seated on a throne, accompanied by four attendants. Other decorative motifs include floriate arches, two birds and, along the inner rim-edge, an abstract design of blue-gray, white and brown, probably derived from script. There is an inscription on the outside of the bowl. The bowl is painted in polychrome enamel with

71

Ewer
Persia (Iran); early thirteenth century
Brass, inlaid with silver; height 16 1/2".
49.1901
Holmes Collection.

gilding on white ground; but, typical of the early Minai ware, the colors —
purple, green, blue and gray — are soft and muted. The piece does not
have a glazed sheen, but the surface shows a smooth and fine texture. Such
Minai wares not only re-established Rayy's pre-eminence as a center of
ceramics in the twelfth–thirteenth centuries, but they are also important
for the development of Persian miniature painting. There seems little doubt
that the early miniaturists were well acquainted with the figural style of
Minai ceramics.

EWER.
The body of this imposing ewer is fluted in ten vertical lobes and richly inlaid with silver. The high, curling lip spout has a hinged cover and the sides
of the neck show crouching lions with fully rounded heads. Below, the
raised ring of silver is decorated with lions chasing hares. Harpies back to
back ornament the rim, and musicians, the shoulder. Around the body is
a frieze of arch-shaped medallions with festival scenes; on the neck and the
base is a benedictory Nashki inscription. The delicacy of the design and
the refinement of the technique make this one of the finest examples of
Islamic inlaid metalwork.

72

The Battle of Alexander With the Dragon
Persia (Iran), Mongol period;
fourteenth century
Leaf of a Shāhnāma. Detail.
Gouache on paper; 7″ × 11 1/2″.
30.105
Ross Collection.

On page 74:

'ABDULLAH IBN AL-FADL
Leaf of Arabic translation of the "Materia Medica" of Dioscorides
Iraq, Baghdad; A.D. 1224
Gouache on paper; 10″ × 13″.
14.536
Goloubew Collection,
Francis Bartlett Donation of
1912, and Picture Fund.

THE BATTLE OF ALEXANDER WITH THE DRAGON.

This leaf with its miniature is from a manuscript of the Persian epic, the Shāhnāma, popularly known as the "Demotte" Shāhnāma. The legend above the miniature reads: "Combat of Alexander and the Rhinoceros." The dragon, a composite of rhinoceros, wolf, lion and eagle, is an inventive elaboration of the text's description of a fire-breathing creature. Alexander, followed by his army, is about to strike the dragon. The landscape, derived from Sung sources in China, is nonetheless Iranian in feeling; while the figures and the color reflect a knowledge of Mesopotamian and Byzantine models. These influences are assimilated into an original, dramatic style worthy of the heroic theme. This and other illustrations of the Demotte Shāhnāma constitute the greatest works of fourteenth-century Persian painting.

'ABDULLAH IBN AL–FADL. *Leaf of Arabic Translation of the "Materia Medica" of Dioscorides.*

p. 74

Two physicians (apothecaries) stand on either side of a large jar, discussing the preparation of medicine. Both are provided with halos; one wears blue robes, the other, red. To judge from the large number of illustrated copies in existence, the *Materia Medica* treatise was popular with the Arabs. Although their strongly figurative style can be traced to Hellenistic and Byzantine models, the delineation in these illustrations is more lively. Since their function was purely "explanatory," the composition is simple and the bold colors make a direct visual appeal.

73

خذ آنا فصب فيه خلا جاد صاف ثم علق الصاصر فيه و لا
سلغ الخل ثم طن فم الانا وقره اما ثم انفخ فيه فان كان فيه

صلاح للاسفنج

استرخا فاجرده ثم ارفعك حتى لا يبقى منه شئ واذا اردت
جعله اقرصه فاعجن بخل حامض ثم يبسه في الشمس الحاره
فانه يكون ابيض بالغ وحرقته ان يأخذ خزفه جديد ثقيق
ويفرشه عليها في برمه وهي على جمر ثم حركه فاذا اتلونه
مثل الرماد فارفعه وبرده وهو يغسل مثل غسل القدميه طبيعته
بارده موافق للعصارات ياكل اللحم الميت ثلث شمع ولادهان

EGYPT
GREECE
ROME

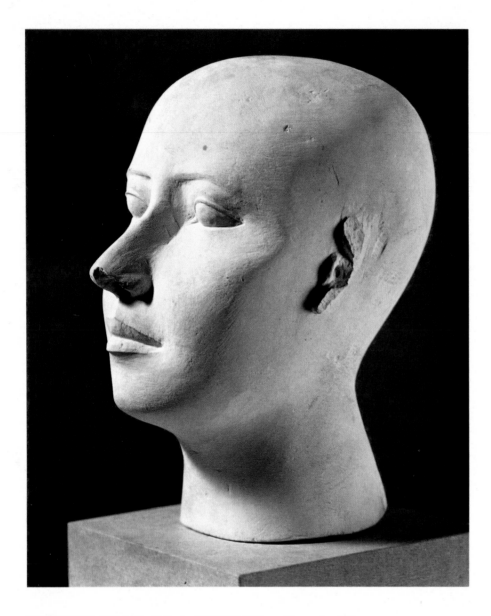

Reserve Head of a Princess
Dynasty IV; circa 2600–2500 B.C.
Limestone; height 10 1/2".
21.328
Harvard-Boston expedition.

RESERVE HEAD OF A PRINCESS. *Dynasty IV*.

Here we find the broader treatment of planes employed by the earlier of the two Giza schools of sculpture. By emphasizing the joining of the narrow bridge of the nose with the high forehead and deep-set eyes, an impression of piquant individuality is produced. This is one of a group of portrait heads of members of the family of Cheops and Chephren that were placed in the burial chamber of the tomb. It is thought that they were intended as a permanent substitute for this essential part of the body, providing a means of recognition for the returning soul. This would accord with Egyptian beliefs concerning the fluidity of interchange between various emanations of the spirit in afterlife and its former material form.

BUST OF PRINCE ANKH–HAF. *Dynasty IV*.

This unusual sculpture, in the form of a bust, is one of the most remarkable examples of portraiture that has survived from ancient Egypt. It was found, thrown down from a low brick bench, in the outer chapel of the prince's

Bust of Prince Ankh-haf
Dynasty IV; circa 2600–2500 B.C.
Painted limestone; height 20".
27.442
Harvard-Boston expedition.

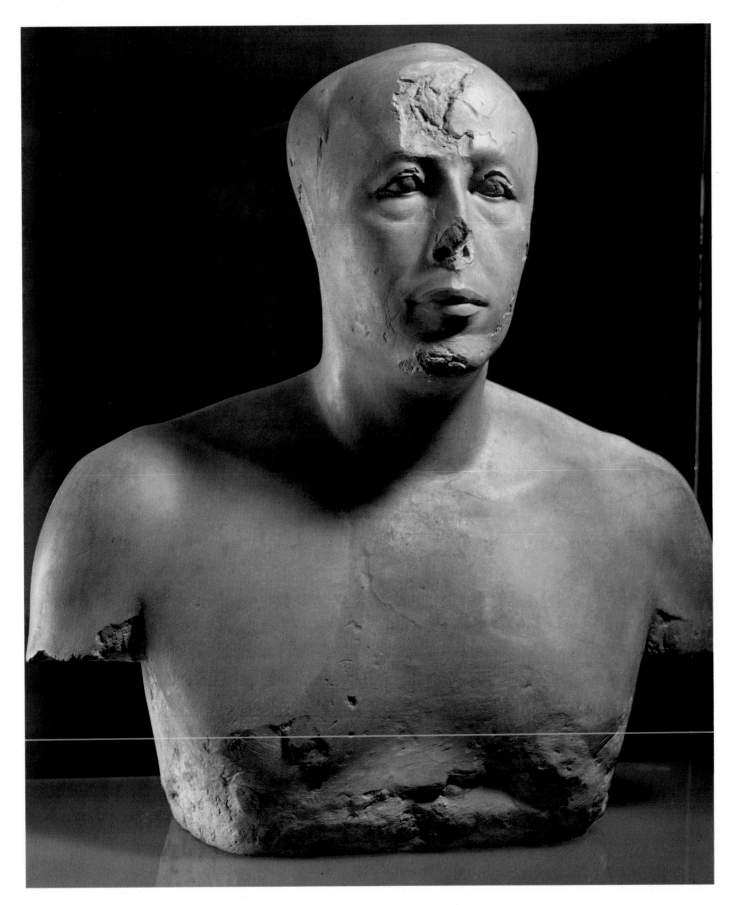

large tomb east of the Great Pyramid at Giza. Although Ankh-haf appears to have served as Vizier to Chephren, the successor of Cheops, he was apparently one of the older members of the royal family and of the same generation as Cheops. The subtle carving of the eyes and mouth, combined with the indication of the bone structure underlying skin and flesh, produces the impression of a living individual, remarkable even among the masterpieces of the Egyptian Old Kingdom.

PAIR STATUE OF KING MYCERINUS AND HIS QUEEN.
Dynasty IV.

Although husband and wife had been pictured together in paintings or relief carvings on the walls of earlier tomb chapels, this well-known statue from the Valley Temple of the Third Pyramid at Giza is the earliest preserved royal example in which the sculptor created a free standing group from a block of hard stone. The back plinth emphasizes the permanence and stability inherent in the divine nature of the monarch. All subordinate detail has been eliminated to convey, through superb modelling, the ultimate in kingly majesty. A human note is contributed by the affectionate gesture of the queen. The statue is the culmination of the artistic skill of the Giza sculptors.

Pair Statue of King Mycerinus and His Queen
Dynasty IV; circa 2600–2500 B.C.
Schist; height 55".
11.1738
Harvard-Boston expedition.

SEATED STATUE OF THE LADY SENNUWY. *Dynasty XII.*

Certainly this is the most appealing of the few large statues of Middle Kingdom ladies. Sennuwy, with her straight, slender figure and calm, sweet expression, exerts an eternal feminine charm. Her husband, Prince Hepzefa, had prepared a large rock-cut tomb at Assiut, where he was governor of the province in Middle Egypt, about halfway between Memphis and Thebes. However, this statue was found in the Sudan, south of the Third Cataract, at the site of an important trading post established early in Dynasty XII. The men of the Middle Kingdom turned to the Pyramid Age for cultural inspiration, as seen in the tomb decorations of the Assiut region. Something of this earlier spirit is to be found in the statue of Sennuwy, as well as the new elements characteristic of the time in which she lived.

Seated Statue of the Lady Sennuwy
Dynasty XII; circa 1950 B.C.
Black granite; height 67 3/4".
14.720
Harvard-Boston expedition.

DEIR EL BERSHEH COFFIN. *Dynasty XII.*

Djehuty-nekht, Governor of the Hare Nome in Middle Egypt, is shown seated, surrounded by elaborately depicted offerings of food and drink. An attendant offers purifying incense. The well-preserved painting is particularly effective against the soft tone of the cedar wood. Obviously, this is the work of one of the great artists of the Middle Kingdom, an innovator whose delicate brushwork captures even the wisp of smoke rising from the burning coals of the censer. The quality of the painting is matched only in a few Twelfth Dynasty tomb chapels, one at Deir el Bersheh and others at Meir, Qau el Qebir and Assiut. However, only limited areas in these wall paintings retain the fresh coloring of the painting illustrated here.

MODEL PROCESSION OF OFFERING BEARERS. *Dynasty XII.*

This group of beautifully carved and painted figures was found with the coffins of Djehuty-nekht and his wife in the burial chamber at Deir el

80

Deir el Bersheh Coffin
Detail.
Dynasty XII; circa 1870 B.C.
Painting on wood; width 15 3/4".
20.1822
Harvard-Boston expedition.

Bersheh. The delicate workmanship is closely related in style and quality to that of the painter of the coffins. Other groups of model figures from the tomb chamber, shown engaged in the activities of a great estate, are more roughly carved. As in the case of the inner coffin of the owner and the outer and inner coffins of his wife, it is evident that workmen other than the master artist himself were employed in Djehuty-nekht's workshops.

RELIEF OF KING AY. *Dynasty XVIII.* *p. 82*

The figure, carved in sunk relief, is one of a pair of Nile Gods tying together the plants of Upper and Lower Egypt as a symbol of the joining of the two lands. It formed part of the side of the throne of a shattered colossal seated figure of Ay, the successor of Tutankhamen. The statue was one of a pair in the king's funerary temple in western Thebes. There are traces of the style of the Amarna Period, particularly in the face of this relief figure. It is

Model Procession of Offering Bearers
Dynasty XII; circa 1870 B.C.
Painted wood; length of base 26 1/4″.
21.326
Harvard-Boston expedition.

not unlike portraits of the young Tutankhamen, whom Ay had supported on the throne. Ay's statues were usurped by Horemheb, Ay's successor at the end of Dynasty XVIII.

TORSO OF KING HAKER. *Dynasty XXIX.*
This is one of the rare monuments of the second king of Dynasty XXIX, who freed Egypt from Persian rule. Considering the magnificent modelling of the body, it is to be regretted that the head is missing. The head would also be a valuable aid in dating other royal sculpture of the Late Period. The Titulary of Haker is inscribed on the back plinth. With the monuments of Nectanebo I and II of Dynasty XXX — before the Persian kings re-established control over Egypt — this torso is one of a group of well-dated works that prove the extraordinarily high quality of Egyptian sculpture before the time of the conquest of Alexander.

Relief of King Ay
Dynasty XVIII; circa 1342 B.C.
Alabaster; height 18".
50.3789
Gift of Edward Valdo Forbes.

Torso of King Haker
Dynasty XXIX; 392–380 B.C.
Gray granite; height 43 3/4″.
29.732
Evans Foundation.

Head of the Sumerian Ruler Gudea
circa 2100 B.C.
Diorite; height 9".
26.289
Francis Bartlett donation, 1912.

HEAD OF THE SUMERIAN RULER GUDEA.

Gudea was governor of the city-state of Lagash in lower Mesopotamia in the period following the collapse of the Akkadian Empire established by Sargon of Akkad, which was contemporary with the late Old Kingdom in Egypt. Gudea's sculptor would therefore have worked at a time when Egypt was undergoing economic collapse, between the end of the flourishing Old Kingdom and the rise of the Middle Kingdom. This head is one of the splendid creations of the very different Mesopotamian style that had developed in the Sargonid period, based on earlier Sumerian sculpture. Gudea's able architects and sculptors employed it to embellish the city of Lagash.

SNAKE GODDESS.

This ivory statuette of a woman holding a pair of hooded snakes may represent a goddess (the classical goddess of harvests and fertility, or the mother-goddess of the principal mountain of Crete) or merely a lady of King Minos' court. She wears the courtly costume of Knossos: her flounced skirt is bounded by thin bands of gold; her bodice is open just above the waist, giving prominence to her breasts. Her nipples, the buttons of the bodice, and her armbands are indicated in gold. She originally wore a high headdress and a gold-studded diadem. The face has a gay, light-hearted quality. Calligraphy and volume are here combined in relaxed, pleasing fashion in pose, profile and small details.

Snake Goddess
Minoan, circa 1500 B.C.
Ivory and gold; height 6 1/2".
The statuette, made at the height of Minoan civilization, was discovered near the palace of Knossos in Crete and brought to the United States early in the twentieth century. The fragments were restored by William J. Young, head of the research laboratory of the Museum.

THE A.D. PAINTER. *Attic Black-figured Hydria.*

The hydria or waterjug is perhaps the grandest of all Greek vases, with its large lip, curling rear handle, saucy side handles, billowing body, and flat shoulder above, curved foot below. The hydria, used to bring water from the communal fountain to the home, shared the universal Greek ability to combine practicality with beauty. The scene on the front of this vase, a direct tribute to its use, is the Doric architecture of a nymphaeum or fountain house, within elaborate borders of palmettes and a fret or maeander. The water flows from five spouts in the form of animals' heads; a lion's head adorns the left wall of the building's interior, matched on the opposite side by the long-eared head of a donkey. Ranged along the back wall are three heads of leopards or panthers, one between each intercolumnation. Five well-attired Athenian women are seen filling their hydriae; from their attitudes, it is evident that a visit to the watering hole was an enjoyable activity. The shoulder of the hydria, being both flat in this instance and, naturally curved, is difficult to utilize; however, artists found that scenes of horses or racing chariots, such as in this piece, suited the area well.

A DIVINE CONTEST AND ATTENDANTS.

This three-sided relief is one of the major sculptural monuments in the severe and contained transitional style between the Archaic period and the Golden Age of the Parthenon. Archaic fussiness of drapery has given way to a smoothed-down, simplified, and severe costume for the women. Hair is more natural, a simple band containing wavy strands rather than corkscrew curls. The relaxed posture of the male nude presages the classical representation of gods and athletes. The figures do not stand or sit stiffly; they now recline on pillows or bend in slight suggestions of activity or emotion. On the central panel (below, left), the winged youth with his curious, post-Archaic smile is thought to be Thanatos, god of death, weighing or judging the qualities of a human soul. The woman on the left may be Aphrodite, and the dejected female on the right, Persephone. The scene may therefore de-

A Divine Contest and Attendants
Greece, circa 470 — 460 B.C.
Three-sided relief
Marble; length 38″.
This is the famous "Boston Throne," so-called because of its resemblance to a chair or seat. With its counterpart, it may have served as the ends of the balustrades flanking an altar, probably dedicated to the regenerative qualities of Aphrodite. Probably from southern Italy; discovered in Rome with its counterpart (now in the Museo Nazionale, Rome).
08.205
Pierce Foundation.

pict a contest between the goddesses of love and the underworld for the soul of Adonis. On one short side (below, center), a reclining youth strums on a large lyre. His proportions, such as the shortness of legs from knee to ankle and the extreme length of his thighs, suggest the slight provincialisms that dominated Greek sculpture in southern Italy at the time. On the other short side (below, right), an old woman — her simple costume and short, un-waved hair indicating that she is probably a servant — sits holding in her raised right hand an object that has been chiselled away. Indeed, the truncated dimensions of this side suggest extensive damage. The woman is un-usual in Greek art, for her face and hunched posture betray the first representation of old age surviving in monumental sculpture. The wrinkles on her face are treated in stylized fashion; they cover the face evenly.

Earring with Winged Charioteer
Greece, fourth century B.C.
Gold; height 2".
The earring, too large for a human ear, may have adorned an oversized cult-statue; or, it may have been a votive offering or deposit in a funerary tomb. It was found in the nineteenth century, probably in a tomb, on the island of Euboea off the coasts of Boeotia and Attica, near the classical city of Eretria. The earring was stolen from the Museum in 1963, in what was at the time America's greatest theft of art from a major museum. It was recovered in 1964.
98.788
Pierce Foundation.

EARRING WITH WINGED CHARIOTEER.

This golden masterpiece is one of the largest and most perfect examples of three-dimensional jewelry from the classic period of Greek art. A goddess in long, flowing chiton or tunic drives a pair of spirited steeds heavenward. A large palmette and a snake serve as the transitional ornament from the loop in the top of the charioteer's head to the object or area from which the earring once hung. Costume, hair style, wings, and countless parallels on other art objects suggest that the figure is Nike, patroness of victory and of charioteers, and symbol of the victory of the human spirit in the afterlife. Another interpretation, based on Plato's writings, suggests that the goddess may be Psyche, symbol of the human soul's eternal quest.

"BARTLETT" APHRODITE.

This head of Aphrodite, goddess of love and beauty, is one of the few surviving sculptures from the workshop of Praxiteles, creator of the Greek ideal of classic female beauty. The hair style, a kind of tentative topknot, serves to date the statue in the last decades of the master or in the era of his immediate followers. The marble seems to have a skin, relatively smooth for the flesh and roughened into textures of depth for the hair. The crystalline core

On page 92:
Man of the Roman Republic (circa 50 B.C.)
Terracotta; height 14".
Discovered about 1895 in excavations near Cumae, northwest of the Bay of Naples.
1.80008
From the collection of Edward Perry Warren.

of the marble gives the stone a background and depth, a perfect foil for the outward softness. The eyes impart an air of cloudy, indefinite mystery.

ARSINOË II OF EGYPT.

This bronze represents a Macedonian or Greek princess of the early Hellenistic period. Although some scholars dispute the identification, it may be a portrait of Arsinoë II, wife of Lysimachus of Thrace and later of Ptolemy II Philadelphus, Macedonian king of Egypt. The queen has highly individual features: a longish nose, thin lips, and a determined expression.

MAN OF THE ROMAN REPUBLIC. p. 92

This is one of the few surviving Roman terracotta portrait-busts. The Romans were not concerned with the Greek ideal of human perfection in a timeless universe; rather, they depicted specific people from known places. This portrait of a sixty-year-old man is both true to life and ideal. It was made by placing wet plaster on the subject's face, forming a life-mask that made possible unusual accuracy and vividness. Hair and other details were no doubt freely rendered by eye, giving a total impression of immediate personality and general, sophisticated dignity.

EUROPE
AMERICA

Curtain or Hanging
Fragment.
Eastern Mediterranean,
late fifth or sixth century A.D.
Wool and linen; 6'2" × 36 3/4".
57.180
Charles Potter Kling Fund.

CURTAIN OR HANGING.

The pattern is woven into this tapestry with brightly colored, fine woolen yarns. It shows a blond man in an elaborate costume standing behind a column and reaching in front of it to pull back a curtain. The two columns, both richly decorated, support an arch decorated with a fruit-pattern. The man seems to be hanging in space, high above the level of the column bases. This curious effect is probably a result of the designer's attempt to represent depth by means of an undeveloped system of linear perspective. The drawing and shading of the pink bands on the curtain suggest that he was trying to convey the idea it was not simply a flat curtain with a pattern of blue and white stripes, but rather was hanging in vertical pleats or folds, with planes of reflected light and shadow. (A.S.C.)

OLIPHANT.

During the Middle Ages, elephant tusks were imported in great quantity from India and Africa to Italy to be fashioned into hunting and signal horns as well as drinking vessels. This magnificent example served the latter purpose and was in all likelihood a so-called tenure horn, symbolizing and testifying to the legal transfer of land. Shrouded in legend and connected with the names of saints or secular lords, these oliphants were often given to Christian churches to be used as containers of relics. Their decoration exercised a powerful influence on the artistic imagination of Romanesque craftsmen.

Except for two sections left plain for the metal mounts (now lost) on which the iron hanging-chain was fastened, the entire surface of this horn is decorated with deeply-cut reliefs depicting beasts and other subjects derived chiefly from classical and early Christian art and iconography. The main subjects are centaurs, peacocks, eagles with splayed wings, sphinxes, griffins, lions, unicorns, bulls and dogs, either locked in combat or confronting one another in pairs separated by stylized trees or the Fountain of Life. Their tails are often animal-headed or terminate in floral tassels; between their legs often appear space-filling plants or the upper parts of other beasts. Some monsters swallow the ends of their own tails which are curled, like snakes, around their necks. (H.S.)

Oliphant
Italy, Salerno (?), circa 1100
Ivory
Length 26″; oval of mouthpiece
5″ to 4 1/2″.
57.581
Maria Antoinette Evans Fund.

CHRIST IN MAJESTY WITH SCENES OF THE OLD AND NEW TESTAMENTS.

The iconography of this fresco is based on a parallel between the Old and New Testaments, a favored scheme in Romanesque decoration and one frequently encountered in the Catalan region. This region was the most important oasis of Roman painting in Spain during the early years of the twelfth century, not only for the great number of monuments, but also for the originality of its highly calligraphical stylization of a typically Western tradition.

The upper half-shell of the apse is filled with the image of Christ in Majesty enclosed within an almond-shaped cloud against a starry backdrop, and flanked by the symbols of the four Evangelists and the Seven Lamps. Below a thick meander-like frieze rendered in perspective, the absidal cylinder is decorated with two bands of figures: those of the Apostles between the windows, and, underneath, the damaged remains of scenes from the Birth of Christ (the *Visitation,* the *Nativity,* the *Annunciation to the Shepherds,* etc.). The decoration is completed on the inner arches of the small windows with the Atlantids supporting the Firmament to the left; the *Sacrifice of Cain and Abel* in the center; and the *Punishment of Cain* to the right. (G.L.M.)

Christ in Majesty with Scenes of the Old and New Testaments
Catalonian; twelfth century
Detached fresco; 22′ × 24′.
Transferred from the apse of the church of Santa Maria de Mur, in the Diocese of Urgel in the vicinity of Lerida, Catalonia; there remains *in situ* a minor apse with traces of a fresco in the *Annunciation.* The church belonged to a Benedictine monastery founded by Raymondo II, count of Pallars; it was built and consecrated in 1069, with amazing rapidity for the times.
21.1285
Maria Antoinette Evans Fund.

Right: detail.

VIRGIN AND CHILD.

The compelling simplicity of volume, vigorous massiveness and outward thrust of the body beneath the drapery of this statue indicate a stylistic similarity to contemporary carvings. Exceptional only is the detailed and articulated treatment of the back of the Madonna. The unknown artist, breaking the confinement of Romanesque stylistic laws, has created a sculpture in the round. The composition, in which the heads of Mother and Child are drawn closely together with the Child's arms around her neck; the almond-shaped eyes, long nose, and veil worn beneath the mantle of the Mother; the hair of the old-looking Child with his bald temples — all belong to a well-known Byzantine type, Glykophylousa, i.e., Sweetly-loving Mother of God. But it would be difficult to find in Byzantine art such dynamic force and violence of affection as seen here. (H.S.)

ARNOLFO DI CAMBIO. *Deacon and Acolytes.*

The three addorsed youthful clerics grouped around a slender column illustrated here, with its companion in the Museo Nazionale, Florence, were part of the Arca of St. Dominic in San Domenico Maggiore, Bologna. The Deacon, distinguished by tunic and maniple, holds the cushion for kneeling upon or supporting the Missal on the altar; the others each carry the pyx and cruet for the wine or water. The spirit and style represent the union of the classical tradition and contemporary Gothic style. (H.S.)

Above, left:
Virgin and Child
Lombardo-Emilian, late twelfth century
Polychromed limestone
Height 29″, length 15 3/4″, diameter 8 1/2″.
Stylistically, this statue belongs to a school active in the late twelfth century, and is closely related to the work of Benedetto Antelami.
57.583
Maria Antoinette Evans Fund.

Above, right:
ARNOLFO DI CAMBIO
Colle Val d'Elsa, circa 1245 —
Florence 1310
Deacon and Acolytes (1264–67)
Marble
47.1290
Grace M. Edwards Fund.

Virgin and Child
Detail.
Ile-de France, circa 1200
Polychromed and gilt oak
Height 61″, width 21 3/4″, diameter 17 3/4″.
59.701
Francis Warden Fund.

98

VIRGIN AND CHILD.

p. 99

The highly developed drapery style of this statue, with its undulating, deep-
cut folds, is a chief feature of the monumental cathedral sculpture of the Ile-
de-France during the period of Philippe-Auguste (1180–1223). Certain
figures on the north transept of Chartres Cathedral, distinguished by the

100

DUCCIO DI BUONINSEGNA
Siena 1255 — Siena 1319
Crucifixion (circa 1305–07)
Tempera on panel
Center 24″ × 15 1/2″;
left and right 17 3/4″ × 7 1/2″.
In the W. Y. Ottley collection in the
eighteenth century; later in the
collection of J. P. Morgan.
45.880
Grant Walker and Charles P. Kling Funds.

same integration of vertical and horizontal elements, may have been designed, if not actually carved, by the master of the Boston *Virgin*. His individual style may also be recognized in fragmentary stone sculptures in Rouen and in Amiens Cathedral. The unknown artist created in this statue an artistically superb and timeless symbol of the universal theme of Mother and Child as a revelation of the divine in nature. And he also realized the discovery of a new aspect of religious art that brought a reconciliation to the chasm between the spiritual and physical worlds pervading the Romanesque. He gave the frozen, hieratic and immobile cult-image of the Madonna organic life, by endowing it with grace and serenity. (H.S.)

DUCCIO DI BUONINSEGNA. *Crucifixion.*

Duccio, founder of the Sienese School and one of the greatest medieval painters, brought to the formal Byzantine tradition a tender emotionalism, a sense of drama, and a feeling for poetical beauty expressed in jewel-like color and sensitive line. Byzantine ritualism is evident in the prescribed gold ground, the compacted figures, and the Pantocrator flanked by angels in the apex of this triptych. But Duccio's sense of drama and excitement animates the crowds at the foot of the cross. The artist's sense of emotion is alive in the beauty of the faces and the poignancy of the expressions of the Virgin and her companions. Sts. Nicholas and Gregory, in the side panels, were probably painted by Simone Martini, Duccio's brilliant pupil and follower. (P.T.R.)

ANONYMOUS BOHEMIAN ARTIST. *Death of the Virgin. p. 102*

The profound religious spirit and mystic intensity of this painting, as well as its dramatic power, are traits that made the Bohemian School famous in the fourteenth century. The subject of the painting derives from the iconography of the Eastern Church. It represents the Virgin in death lying upon a bier and attended by Christ who with one hand pronounces a benediction and with the other cradles the departed soul of the Virgin, personified by a tiny child. A band of clouds separates Him from the twelve grieving Apostles who press tightly around the bier; one Apostle reaches upward to sound the death knell.

The nameless artist of this rare painting has organized his space according to the rules of perspective that, together with the plastic modelling of the heads, figures, and the realistic differentiation of types, shows the enlivening influence of contemporary Italian painting, especially that of Siena. The monk, in smaller scale, kneeling at the foot of the bier is probably the donor of the painting, while the two women, also in small scale, are probably related to the scene, but in a way no longer clear. (P.T.R.)

ANONYMOUS BOHEMIAN ARTIST
Death of the Virgin (circa 1350)
Oak covered with canvas; 39 3/8″ × 28″.
Part of a larger work, perhaps a
polytych, now lost.
William F. Warden Fund and by exchange.

DONATELLO. *The Madonna in the Clouds.*

This little masterpiece is less well-known and, unjustly, less appreciated than the other, larger marble reliefs by Donatello carved in the sketchy technique called *rilievo schiacciato*. It is exceptional in the originality of the interpretation of an established theme — the Madonna of Humility — as well as in the highly personal, spontaneous, and daringly free style of its execution. The modelling has the smooth but sure touch of a silverpoint drawing, and the seemingly simple design surprises by its correct perspective projections and radical foreshortenings. The *schiacciato* technique as well as the transfer of the earth-bound to a "celestial" Madonna of Humility, elevated like an *assunta* to the skies and surrounded by winged angels and cherubs,

DONATELLO
Florence 1386 — Florence 1466
The Madonna in the Clouds
Marble; 13″ × 12 1/2″.
17.1470
Gift of Quincy A. Shaw through
Quincy A. Shaw, Jr. and
Marian Shaw Houghton.

GIOVANNI DI PAOLO
Siena 1403 — Siena 1482
The Virgin of Humility
Tempera on panel; 22″ × 17″.
Another version is in the Pinacoteca
of Siena.
30.772
Maria Antoinette Evans Fund.

MASTER OF THE
BARBERINI PANELS
(GIOVANNI ANGELO
D'ANTONIO DA CAMERINO?)
Presentation of the Virgin in the Temple
Second half of the fifteenth century
Tempera on panel; 58″ × 38 1/2″.
This panel originally came from the Ducal
Palace of Urbino where, along with other
panels that probably illustrated other epi-
sodes in the life of the Virgin, it was part
of the decoration of a room, perhaps the
Alcove of Federico da Montelfeltro which
still exists in the palace.
37.108
Charles Potter Kling Fund.

are both Donatello's own inventions. Certain details may indicate the influence of Michelozzo, with whom Donatello collaborated until 1438, and
thus would suggest a date for the relief in the late 1430s.

From Vasari we learn that the relief belonged to the Florentine Pugliese
family, and that around 1500 Piero del Pugliese had it enshrined in a
wooden tabernacle with movable wings, painted on both sides by Fra Bar-
tolommeo. (The wings, depicting the *Annunciation,* the *Nativity,* and the
Circumcision, are today in the Uffizi Gallery.) (H.S.)

GIOVANNI DI PAOLO. *The Virgin of Humility.*
Of the Sienese painters active around the middle of the fifteenth century,
Giovanni di Paolo remains an enigmatic personality although his works are
many and familiar. While his contemporary Sano di Pietro continued the
monotonous reproduction of the Madonnas consecrated as icons a century
earlier by Sienese masters, Giovanni di Paolo attempted to bring up to date,
with a calligraphic, tormented style, the visionary fantasy that had constituted the ultimate dream-world of the art produced in the courts of Europe
for almost a century.

This *Madonna and Child* goes beyond the scope of mere revelation of the
mystery of the Divine Conception to attempt a more complex interpretation
of the medieval idea of the *mappamundus volubilis.* This cosmic vision is
presented according to the archaic scheme of the universe composed of con-
centric spheres, illustrated by parallel arches that lead the eye to a distant
horizon. The background contains an encyclopedic variety of natural phe-
nomena, from flowered meadows in the foreground, to woods, mountains,
tiny buildings, and the sea, dotting the landscape. Against this tapestry-like
background, the figure of the Madonna is projected like a phantasmagoric
shadow over the world. (G.L.M.)

MASTER OF THE BARBERINI PANELS.
Presentation of the Virgin in the Temple.
The authorship of this delicate painting was the object of a fascinating study
by Federico Zeri (*Due dipinti, la filologia e un nome,* Torino, 1961), in
which he was able to identify the artist with a historically documented person. From the group of works associated with this personality there emerges
a figurative culture formed on the example of Domenico Veneziano's activity in Perugia, as well as Filippo Lippi's production during the years
1447 to 1450, and contemporary painting in centers such as Camerino and
Rimini. The artist's most important enterprise seems to have been his par-
ticipation in the decoration of the Ducal Palace of Urbino, of which the
only known remains are the present panel and its companion-piece in the
Metropolitan Museum, once in the Barberini Gallery in Rome. It is surprising to note how well documents of the life of the painter Giovanni Angelo d'Antonio from Camerino in the Marche region of Italy correspond
with the stylistic traits of this hitherto anonymous artist. (G.L.M.)

ROGIER VAN DER WEYDEN. *St. Luke Painting the Virgin.*

This famous work, one of the most important Flemish paintings in America, is thought to have been created as the altarpiece for the Chapel of the Painters Guild in Brussels. Van der Weyden moved to Brussels in 1435 from his native Tournai and was named official painter to the city. It is not known how the painting was brought to Spain, nor when and how it found its way into the renowned collection of Don Sebastian Borbon y Braganza. It was presented to the Boston Museum in 1893 and thus became the first important Flemish painting to enter an American public collection. The painting was copied at least three times (one is in the Hermitage, Leningrad; another is in the Alte Pinakothek, Munich), and van der Weyden's Madonna type was so admired that it appeared and reappeared in the works of lesser artists throughout the century.

The painting illustrates the charming apocryphal story that St. Luke, in addition to his skill as a doctor, was also an artist who painted a portrait of the Virgin. Van der Weyden depicted the scene in a prosperous burgher's house of the time. Here a throne has been improvised from a bench and a piece of brocade suspended from the rafters. Light pours in through an open loggia which overlooks a town situated on the banks of a broad river. Against the rectangular structuring of the space design, van der Weyden placed the figures of the Virgin and Child and St. Luke, with his characteristic grace of movement and tenderness of feeling. The face of St. Luke may be an idealized likeness of van der Weyden himself.

While the painting is entirely realistic in outward appearance — no haloes or other supernatural signs of sanctity are permitted — it abounds in symbolism. For example, carved on the arm of the bench are the naked Adam and Eve, signifying the Fall of Man for whose redemption the Saviour was born. The loggia has a triple-opening signifying the Trinity; likewise, the circular window above has three divisions. On the desk under the window lies an open book, symbol of Luke's calling as an Evangelist. And, deeply shadowed under the desk lest its presence disturb the illusion of reality, crouches an ox, the apocalyptic symbol of St. Luke. (P.T.R.)

THE MARTYRDOM OF SAINT PAUL. *p. 108*

The beheading of Saint Paul, at a place outside Rome, is the subject of this tapestry. A group of pagans surround the Emperor Nero (in golden armor) at the left; a group of Christians stand at the right. The tapestry shows how, according to legend, milk rather than blood spurted from the saint's severed neck, and how at each of the three points that his head touched after the execution, a spring appeared in the earth. Near the saint's head, a Latin inscription reads, "for me life is Christ and death is gain." At the top, above a representation of God the Father and the soul of the saint (shown as a child borne heavenward by angels in a sheet) is a scroll inscribed in French:

ROGIER VAN DER WEYDEN
Tournai circa 1399 — Brussels 1464
St. Luke Painting the Virgin
Painted on oak; 54 1/4" × 48 7/8".
Probably painted in
van der Weyden's early period.
93.153
Gift of Mr. and Mrs. Henry Lee Higginson.

106   *Right:* detail.

Cõmcut laint pol a efte decole hors rõine
ca telte feparee du cor ps fift troip caulp

"How Saint Paul was beheaded outside Rome. His head separated from the body, made three jumps." Eight small scrolls, inscribed "Peace" in French, appear near the outer edges of the composition.

The coat of arms shown in the upper left and lower right corners of the tapestry is that of Guillaume de Hellande. The coat of arms shown in the opposite corners is that of the Bishopric of Beauvais. Guillaume de Hellande, Bishop of Beauvais from 1444 to 1462, commissioned a set of tapestries of the *Life of Saint Peter* for the Cathedral of Beauvais in 1460. This tapestry was the next to the last one in that series. (A.S.C.)

The Martyrdom of Saint Paul
France or the Franco-Flemish territories, circa 1460
Tapestry
Wool, silk and metallic yarns;
9'4 1/2" ×6'8 3/4".
38.758
Francis Bartlett Fund.

CHRIST BEFORE PILATE.

This tapestry is associated with a series of tapestry-designs depicting the history of the Passion of Christ. The complete piece shows six episodes in that narrative, brilliantly composed within a complex arrangement of architectural units. The scenes depicted are: Christ standing before Pilate (detail shown here); Herod and his men mocking Christ; Judas bringing the thirty pieces of silver to the chief priests and elders; Christ before Pilate once more; Christ crowned with thorns and mocked; and Christ presented to the crowd. Other tapestries and embroideries, woven after this series of compositions, and preserved in European collections, repeat the left or right halves of this composition and also show that the scheme for the series in-

Christ Before Pilate
Detail.
Tapestry
Wool and silk; 13'8 1/4" × 29'7".
29.1046
Gift of Robert Treat Paine II in
memory of his son, Walter Cabot Paine.

cluded at least eleven other episodes. This tapestry hung in the chapel at Knole, Kent. According to tradition, it was taken to Knole in the first half of the sixteenth century either by Archbishop Warham or by Archbishop Cranmer. (A.S.C.)

ANONYMOUS FLEMISH ARTIST.

The Martyrdom of Saint Hippolytus.

This great work of early Flemish art, flawlessly preserved, was unknown until its appearance on the French art market in 1962. The master who created it remains unidentified. It is known, however, for whom the triptych was painted. The exteriors of the side panels (not shown here) are painted in grisaille with representations of four saints tentatively identified as St. Bavo of Ghent, St. Elizabeth of Hungary, St. Thomas à Becket, and St. Catherine, and the arms of Hippolytus de Barthoz and his wife, Elizabeth van Keverwyck. Berthoz was financial advisor to Philip the Good of Burgundy and a few years earlier had commissioned Dirk Bouts to paint the well-known triptych that celebrates the martyrdom of his patron saint.

While the painter remains anonymous, it is evident that he belonged to the School of Ghent and was closely related to Hugo van der Goes. Van der

ANONYMOUS FLEMISH ARTIST
The Martyrdom of Saint Hippolytus
(circa 1480)
Oil on panel; 39 1/2″ × 9′7″ overall.
63.660
Walter M. Cabot Fund.

Goes' influence is strong; he may even have created the unusual composition, which is clearly the work of an innovator. Moreover, a previous tie to van der Goes is significant: Berthoz convinced him to paint wings for the Bouts triptych, using the family patron saints and arms as subjects. In this painting, the astounding centrifugal movement of the central composition radiates across the separations of the panels, reaching to the limits of the three-part painting, so that two of the executioners with their straining horses become the principal subjects of the wings. The stature of the artist is confirmed not only by the originality of his dynamic design, but by the note of transcendence that is central to it. Hippolytus is pictured in a way that recalls the crucified Christ, his body seemingly illuminated from within while his ecstatic expression tells us that he already sees the heavenly host. The brutality of this rare subject is further mitigated by the bright and decorative color, principally a harmony of blue and red, by the enchanting landscape and the profusion of flowers blossoming in the foreground, by the gorgeous costumes of courtiers and horsemen rendered with the painstaking perfection of Flemish masters. (P.T.R.)

LUCAS VAN LEYDEN. *Moses Striking the Rock*.   *p. 112*
The subject of this painting is not only characteristic of Lucas but also prophetic of the development of Dutch painting. It heralds the first stirrings

of genre art, and the transition from a preoccupation with religious inspiration to an absorption with nature and the daily life of man. This scene from Exodus provided a formidable challenge to his narrative genius: Moses, leading the thirsty Jews into the wilderness, beseeches the Lord for help and is told to strike the rock of Horeb with his staff. Water pours forth, which the Israelites eagerly catch in various vessels. Lucas' band of thirty-four Israelites could be so many chatty Dutch burghers. The motley crowd is skillfully integrated with the natural setting of rocks, trees and landscape, generating a moody and poetic atmosphere. (P.T.R.)

GIOVANNI BATTISTA ROSSO. *Dead Christ with Angels.*

Dr. John Shearman of the Courtauld Institute has shown that the subject of this painting is not the familiar one of the dead Christ supported by angels, but rather the extremely subtle theme of Christ reawakening to his second life. The angels are thus observers of the miracle rather than com-

LUCAS VAN LEYDEN
Leyden 1494(?) — Leyden 1533
Moses Striking the Rock (1527)
Tempera on canvas; 72″ × 93″.
This is Lucas' only painting in
tempera on canvas.
Formerly in the
Barbarini Collection, Rome;
later in the German
National Museum, Nurmberg.
54.1432
William K. Richardson Fund.

GIOVANNI BATTISTA ROSSO
(IL ROSSO FIORENTINO)
Florence 1494 — Paris 1540
Dead Christ with Angels
(circa 1525)
Oil on panel; 52 1/2″ × 41″.
Painted for Rosso's close friend and
fellow Florentine, Cardinal Leonardo
Tornabonni, Bishop of Borgo
Sansepolcro in Umbria.
58.527
Charles Potter Kling Fund.

passionate supporters of the lifeless body. The body of Christ, cleansed of the blood of martyrdom, assumes the tensions of a living organism.

Rosso's painting is the most important Mannerist work in America. It reflects the powerful influence of the figure-style of Michelangelo as seen in the Ignudi of the Sistine Ceiling. Characteristically, the spatial design is suppressed and the figures so densely packed within the composition that the lower limbs of Christ seem to project beyond the picture plane. The unconventional color harmonies are also typical of Mannerist painting. (P.T.R.)

TITIAN. *Saint Catherine of Alexandria Adoring the Cross.*

Although attributed to Titian's late period, this painting is not characterized by the loose forms and thick brushstroke typical of the ultimate phase of his career. Considering the rigorous perspective of the architectural setting and the firm plasticity of the forms, it is more probable that it was executed toward the middle of the century.

The pietistic scene takes place in what seems to be the solemn atrium of a Venetian villa of vaguely Palladian design, and thus maintains a certain sense of intimacy in spite of the grandiose, pre-baroque composition. The

TITIAN
(TIZIANO VECELLIO)
Pieve di Cadore circa 1488 — Venice 1576
*Saint Catherine of Alexandria
Adoring the Cross*
Oil on canvas; 37" × 30 1/2".
The sword and the palm are symbols of
her martyrdom by decapitation,
while the classical relief used as the
base of the Crucifixion
represents the Deposition.
48.499
Purchase Fund and Otis Norcross Fund.

perspective focal-point is slightly right of center, in line with the vertical Cross projected picturesquely against the distant landscape. (G.L.M.)

TINTORETTO. *The Nativity.*

In this monumental composition we easily recognize the Virgin and St. Joseph adoring the Christ Child, and the bearded shepherd with his crook. In the distance on the left the Wise Men approach in a cavalcade; on the right, the shepherds in the fields hear the tidings from heaven. The identity of the woman on the right is unknown. Tintoretto may have drawn upon an ancient, discredited legend wherein a midwife attends the Virgin at the Nativity; or the woman may simply be an old shepherdess to whom Tintoretto has given the appearance of a sybil. Her gesture of astonishment implies that she was the first mortal to recognize the miracle of the manger. At any rate, her presence in the scene is one of Tintoretto's daring inventions. Barnyard creatures are introduced for descriptive purposes, but the lamb's awareness of the Christ Child suggests that it serves as the usual symbol of sacrifice. The traditional stable is merely indicated by a few posts and the presence of the ox and ass. The influence of Michelangelo is evident in the modelling of the women and the monumentality of the conception. (P.T.R.)

TINTORETTO
(JACOPO ROBUSTI)
Venice 1518 — Venice 1594
The Nativity (circa 1570)
Oil on canvas; 61″ × 138 1/2″.
46.1430
Gift of Quincy Adams Shaw.

EL GRECO
(DOMENICO THEOTOKOPOULOS)
Crete 1541 — Toledo 1614
Fray Hortensio Felix de Palavicino
(1609)
Oil on canvas;
44 1/2" × 33 3/4".
04.234
Isaac Sweetser Fund.

EL GRECO. *Fray Hortensio Felix de Palavicino.*

Painted in the artist's late maturity, this work reveals El Greco's visionary preoccupation: the corporal presence of the monk seems strangely intangible, suffused with otherworldliness. Greco took full advantage of the dramatic black and white of the Trinitarian habit to set off the head that appears at the apex of a black and white triangle and is further accentuated by the top edge of the chair-back. The subject is Fray Felix (1580–1633), theologian, humanist, and poet. The close friendship between the two men is evident in this sensitive and highly personal portrait. (P.T.R.)

DIEGO VELÁZQUEZ DE SILVA.

Don Baltasar Carlos and His Dwarf.

The subject of this opulent painting is Don Baltasar Carlos, eldest son of

DIEGO VELÁZQUEZ DE SILVA
Seville 1599 — Madrid 1660
Don Baltasar Carlos and His Dwarf
(1631)
Oil on canvas;
53 1/2" × 41".
01.104
Henry Lillie Pierce Fund.

Philip IV and Elizabeth of France. The Infante had been born in the artist's absence and was now almost a year and a half old. Here Velázquez breaks out of the stiff traditional formula for royal portraits and creates a fluid composition in movement and depth. He even permits himself the luxury of playfulness. His infant subject is dressed in a parade doublet, a plate armor collar around his neck. He appears to be moving forward, his hand on the hilt of his sword. In the foreground on a rich cushion lies his stiff leather helmet. Counter-movement is provided by the court dwarf dressed as a child. As the dwarf looks back to regard his royal master, he holds in one hand a rattle, in the other an apple, a playful if not ironic reference to the symbols of kingship, the scepter and the orb. (P.T.R.)

PETER PAUL RUBENS. *The Head of Cyrus Brought to Queen Tomyris.* Rubens painted this monumental work in 1622, while he was working on the series celebrating the life of Marie de' Medici, now in the Louvre. It shows the Queen of the Messegetae celebrating her triumph over the all-powerful Cyrus, King of Persia, by having his head bathed in blood in ful-fillment of her pledge of vengeance for the loss of her son. An extraordinary

PETER PAUL RUBENS
Siegen 1577 — Antwerp 1640
The Head of Cyrus Brought to Queen Tomyris
Oil on canvas; 80 1/2″ × 141″.
41.40
Robert J. Edwards Fund.

assemblage of courtiers in exotic dress attends her. The composition is carried in wave-like rhythm from the sweep of the Queen's train on the left, along the bent back of the half-naked servant, to the curve of the swordsman's scimitar on the right. An autobiographical thread runs through Rubens' art; the two page boys supporting the Queen's train are his sons, Albert and Nicholas. (P.T.R.)

JACOB JORDAENS.   *Double Portrait of a Man and His Wife.*
This beautiful painting makes it clear why Jacob Jordaens became the popular successor as portrait painter in Antwerp of Rubens and Van Dyck, his

JACOB JORDAENS
Antwerp 1593 — Antwerp 1678
Double Portrait of a Man and His Wife
Oil on panel; 48 1/2″ × 36 1/2″.
17.3232
Bequest of Robert Dawson Evans.

120

older and more famous contemporaries. As Rubens' assistant, Jordaens had ample opportunity to study with the master. Indeed, it may be taken as a compliment to this *Double Portrait* that it was long considered the work of Rubens himself.

Direct in conception and full of vitality in its portrayal of two personalities, the painting has the robustness and vigor characteristic of Flemish art in the 17th century. This young couple in their personal pride, self-possession and their patent affluence symbolize the establishment of a powerful bourgeoisie in the Netherlands at the time. (P.T.R.)

REMBRANDT VAN RIJN. *Pastor Johannes Elison.*

Rembrandt was at the pinnacle of youthful success when he painted this portrait of Johannes Elison and a companion portrait of his wife, Maria, leaders of the Dutch colony in Norwich, England. Not content with mere likenesses, Rembrandt raised portraiture to a higher level. In consequence, these life-size portraits are dramatized by light that flows around the figures, describing space and revealing form. The faces of the pastor and his wife show the depth of Rembrandt's psychological penetration of character. (P.T.R.)

JACOB VAN RUISDAEL. *A Rough Sea.*

Jacob van Ruisdael is probably the greatest Dutch landscape painter of the seventeenth century. The grandeur, solemnity, and divine beauty of nature is the inspiration for this awesome view of the estuary of the river Ij outside

Amsterdam. Billowing clouds ride serenely above a dark and troubled sea. Half-appearing on the distant horizon is the perilously low-lying coast, reminder of the everlasting struggle of the Dutch against the power of the sea. The human drama of the encounter is further emphasized by the sailboats bending heavily to the wind; the one in the foreground, pennants flying, moves through deep shadow, its sail revealed for a moment in a ray of sun. Ruisdael's sharp observation is evident in the foreground: the sea is visibly strained by the tug of the tide in one direction and by the whip of the wind in the other. (P.T.R.)

NICOLAS POUSSIN.   *Mars and Venus.*

The two major influences on Poussin were the relics of the classical world of Greece and Rome and the art of Titian. The athletic development, ideal proportions and graceful posturing of the human body in pagan sculpture, and the compositional rhythms of sarcophagus reliefs underlie the art of this great classicist painter. The self-conscious perfection and restraint of the composition as well as the poses of the gods and their attendants in this painting may be inspired by a Roman sarcophagus in the Lateran Museum. Titian's influence finds expression in the vividness of the color, the easy integration of figures and landscape, and above all in the sensuous mood of the scene. Poussin pays direct tribute to the great Venetian by frankly deriving the mischievous cupids (left foreground) from Titian's *Worship of Venus* in the Prado, Madrid. (P.T.R.)

NICOLAS POUSSIN
Les Andelys 1594 — Rome 1665
Mars and Venus (circa 1630)
Oil on canvas; 61″ × 84 1/4″.
40.89
Augustus Hemenway and
Arthur Wheelwright Funds.

122

CLAUDE LORRAIN. *Parnassus.*

Claude brought to landscape a grandeur of form and space and a unity of parts to the whole composition that were unknown before. A true sense of Arcadian poetry characterizes this work as it does his entire *oeuvre*. In *Parnassus,* the subject is more specific than is usually the case: Apollo surrounded by the Muses gathered in the sacred grove, on the slopes of Mt. Helicon. Below lies the Hippocrene spring, the inspiration of poets, alive with graceful swans. The towering trees, majestic distances of hills and sea, and the Ionic temple are brought into a unified vision by Claude's gift of creating an enveloping light. (P.T.R.)

ANTOINE WATTEAU. *La Perspective.* *pp. 124–125*

Antoine Watteau's art was the embodiment of the social ideals of eighteenth-century France: devotion to beauty and refinement, cultivation of gallantry and lighthearted amusement, love of informality. Pompous portraiture and sober paintings inspired by history or the Bible, which symbolized the gloomy, declining court of Louis XIV, were replaced under the regency of the hedonistic Duc d'Orleans by an art entirely new in spirit, an art that celebrated music, love and laughter, picnics and garden parties, the theatre and the dance. The leader in this transformation was Watteau, and though he died in 1721 at an early age, his graceful art was to influence the entire century.

The revival of performances by the Italian Commedia del'arte during the

CLAUDE LORRAIN
Champagne 1600 — Rome 1682
Parnassus (1681)
Oil on canvas; 38 1/2″ × 53 1/4″.
12.1050
Picture Fund, 1912.

regency left an indelible mark on Watteau's art. It inspired the poses of his figures, their movements and grouping. The Commedia stimulated his sense of mime and perhaps even his harmony of composition. *La Perspective* is one of Watteau's most felicitous *fêtes galantes,* a series of paintings inspired by the languorous diversions of the new and privileged society. It was probably painted at Montmorency, the estate of his patron, the great collector, Pierre Crozat, during Watteau's residence there in 1716. (P.T.R.)

GIOVANNI BATTISTA TIEPOLO. *Time Unveiling Truth.* p. 126
Unsurpassed as a master of epic themes and visionary grandeur, Tiepolo painted his greatest works on the ceilings of Europe's palaces. But *Time Unveiling Truth,* perhaps Tiepolo's most monumental easel painting, conveys to an uncommon degree this aspect of his genius. The characters in this classic theme are a muscular, sunburned Father Time, gnarled with age, and his companion, Truth, a proud and splendid young woman. Serenely seated upon his lap, Truth submits to her ceremonious disrobing by Time. His giant wings spell irresistible strength, his lowered head speaks of determination. At his feet are the customary attributes of Chronos: the chariot, the scythe symbolizing death, the infant symbolizing rebirth. Amidst a cascade of gorgeous drapery is a parrot — symbol of the vanity

124

ANTOINE WATTEAU
Valenciennes 1684 — Paris 1721
La Perspective (circa 1716)
Oil on canvas; 18 1/2" × 22".
23.573
Maria Antoinette Evans Fund.

Right: detail.

of human life. Truth, with the face and coiffure of a Venetian beauty, triumphantly dominates the composition, her foot upon the globe, while her symbol, the sun, rides high in the sky.

The painting is dynamic in design and charged with an astonishing plastic force. In his sumptuous color, mastery of drawing, and brilliant brushwork, Tiepolo here surpasses almost every eighteenth-century artist. But the most exciting aspect of the painting is the power of Tiepolo's imagination — his ability to project with perfect mastery and the persuasion of reality what could be only a vision in his mind. (P.T.R.)

CANALETTO. *Bacino di San Marco.*
Of the many practitioners of the art of painting city views, none was more skilled than Canaletto. This magnificent painting of the spacious entrance to Venice, the *Bacino,* reveals Canaletto's ability to unify his subject with a carefully controlled composition of light: to paint a great sweep of space and then enrich it with lavish detail and animate it with human activity. The water traffic is alive with the activity of seamen and gondoliers. The clouds dapple the expanse of water with shadow, suppressing and accenting details and passages of color. (P.T.R.)

JOSEPH EFFNER
Console Table
Munich, Germany, circa 1730
Gilded oak; height 33 1/2",
length 59 1/4", diameter 25 1/2".
57.685
Helen and Alice Colburn Fund.

Below: detail.

FRANÇOIS BOUCHER
Paris 1703 — Paris 1770
The Luncheon (1756)
Tapestry; 11'9 1/2" ×11'1 /4".
Designed by François Boucher;
woven under the directorship of
André-Charlemagne Charron.
40.66
Francis Bartlett Fund.

JOSEPH EFFNER. *Console Table.*   *p. 128*

This richly carved table is decorated with masks on the knees of the cabriole legs, a portrait medallion of the Austrian Princess, Maria Amalia, on the skirt, and seated cupids holding the arms of Austria on the stretcher. Its mate in the Frankfurt Museum is decorated with the arms of Bavaria and a portrait medallion of Elector Karl Albert of Bavaria, who married Maria Amalia in 1726. Both console tables were designed by the great Munich architect Joseph Effner, from engravings by Jean Bernard Toro of Paris. They were executed by the court carpenter, Johann Adolf Pichler, for one of the splendid Bavarian castles, either the Munich Residence, Nymphenburg, or Schleissheim. (H.H.S.)

FRANÇOIS BOUCHER. *The Luncheon.*   *p. 129*

This tapestry shows one of the six subjects comprising the series *La Noble Pastorale* or *Les Beaux Pastorales* which was woven many times at the Beauvais manufactory. Some of the compositions were woven in the form of covers for the backs or seats of chairs or sofas. *The Luncheon* shows two shepherds, two shepherdesses, and three small boys pausing for a meal of grapes in a small clearing in the countryside, at the foot of some masonry ruins. Three sheep appear in the middle distance at the right. The border, designed to resemble a carved and gilded frame, supports at its upper center the coat of arms of France and Navarre surmounted by a royal crown and surrounded by the collars of the Orders of St. Michael and of the Holy Spirit. (A.S.C.)

CLAUDE–NICOLAS LEDOUX. *Wall Panels.*

These are details of two boiseries, from a set of eight made for a salon in the Hotel de Montmorency in Paris. Depicted, in relief, are classical nymphs in the tradition of Jean Goujon, cupids, trophies of arms and musical instruments, and shields with the interlaced initials MO (for Montmorency). They were purchased in Paris about 1840 by Peter Parker of Boston. The panels were sold at auction in 1871. Two opposite pairs were acquired by the Boston Athenaeum, two by the Museum of Fine Arts. (H.S.)

GEORGE ROMNEY. *Anne, Lady de la Pole.*   *p. 132*

George Romney, a newcomer in the art of "face painting," soon outclassed Sir Joshua Reynolds in popularity. Painted at the height of Romney's success, *Anne, Lady de la Pole* is probably his finest work in America. The lady stands with easy grace in a sylvan setting, a favorite foil of English painters. The exaggerated proportions of her long-limbed body, the languor and elegant informality of her pose, the shimmering satin of the drapery,

130

CLAUDE-NICOLAS LEDOUX
Paris 1756 — Paris 1806
Wall Panels (1770–72)
Details.
Carved oak, painted in
watercolors and gilt in gesso;
12′ × 32″.
79.329, 79.326
Right: detail.

132

are all hallmarks of Romney's style. These traits accentuated the aristocratic status of his sitters and contributed to Romney's success in the opulent society of eighteenth-century London. (P.T.R.)

JOHN SINGLETON COPLEY. *Paul Revere.*
Copley, the New England Puritan, placed truth above elegance in portraiture, thus rejecting the artificial conventions he had inherited. His brilliant series of portraits are outstanding in their revelation of human character, their plastic force and originality of design. One of the most notable is that of the famous silversmith and patriot, Paul Revere. With characteristic originality, Copley pictures Revere in shirt sleeves at his bench, as if momentarily interrupted at his work. With one hand he cups his square, rather fleshy face, with the other he grasps a newly-fashioned teapot on a leather hammering-pillow. He is about to begin engraving with the tools that are scattered before him. (P.T.R.)

JOHN SINGLETON COPLEY
Boston 1738 — Boston 1815
Paul Revere (circa 1768–1770)
Oil on canvas; 35″ × 28 1/2″.
30.781
Gift of William B. Joseph and
Edward H. R. Revere.

133

GILBERT STUART. *George Washington.*

This portrait is probably the best-loved painting in America. Known as the "Athenaeum Head," from its purchase by the Boston Athenaeum in 1831, it was the third and last portrait of the first President that Gilbert Stuart painted from life. Commissioned by Mrs. Washington, it was painted either in Stuart's studio in Germantown, Pennsylvania or in the President's home in Philadelphia. With its companion portrait of Martha Washington, the painting remained in Stuart's possession until his death. It thereby served as a model for the many replicas made by Stuart as well as for the almost innumerable copies made by other artists.

When Stuart painted the first President, he was in full control of the fluid,

GILBERT STUART
Narragansett 1755 — Boston 1828
George Washington (1796)
Oil on canvas; 48" × 37".
Ath. 1
Deposited by the Boston Athenaeum.

easy style he had developed in London under the influence of Reynolds and Romney. In his interpretation of Washington, he strove for gravity and suave dignity. He succeeded in creating an image aloof and commanding, strong yet sensitive. While the likeness is appropriately monumental in conception, the unfinished state of the painting lends it an appealing note of informality. (P.T.R.)

JOSEPH MALLORD WILLIAM TURNER. *The Slave Ship.*

One of the most brilliant innovators in the history of painting, Turner took as subject matter the elements themselves and symbolized them in his own personal vocabulary as abstract forces. He conceived of nature in terms of color and light and, in response to the Romantic preoccupation of his era, was concerned with the spectacular aspects of sea and sky and mountain, and the atmospheric drama of snow and wind and rain. Turner's art became increasingly abstract with time. In his later years, light and atmosphere rather than picturesque scenes were the dominant themes of his painting. *The Slave Ship,* one of Turner's most famous works, is a classic

135

example of this later development. The focal point of the heroic seascape is not the ship but the setting sun, and the overriding drama is the symphonic display of sky and sea, not the account of man's bestiality. Turner anticipated the Impressionists in his treatment of light. In *The Slave Ship,* the strongest light — indeed the source of all light, the sun — is placed at the center of the composition.

The painting is based on the story of the slave ship, *Zong.* When an epidemic broke out aboard ship in 1783, the captain cast the slaves overboard since no insurance could be collected for those who died of illness. The English critic, John Ruskin, the first owner of *The Slave Ship,* praised the painting in these words: "I think the noblest sea that Turner ever painted, and if so, the noblest certainly ever painted by man, is that of *The Slave Ship,* the chief Academy picture of the Exhibition of 1840. . . . I believe, if I were reduced to rest Turner's immortality upon any single work, I should choose this." (P.T.R.)

THOMAS SEYMOUR. *Commode.*
Semi-elliptical in plan, the design of this piece relies almost entirely upon applied decoration to achieve its expression. Brass lion's-paw feet support the four turned and carved leg-and-post supports that rise to the top and flank two graduated sections of four swinging hinged compartments and one center panel of four graduated drawers. On the base is a row of carved darts

THOMAS SEYMOUR
Commode (Boston, 1809)
Mahogany, satinwood, bird's-eye maple and rosewood; 41" × 49" × 24 1/4".
23.19
M. and M. Karolik Collection.
Right: detail.

beneath a plain veneered surface, separated from the drawers by a simple molding. Each drawer is veneered in bird's-eye maple and bordered by stringing and cross-banding. The top surface (detail shown here) is divided into seventeen equal segments of mahogany and satinwood. The segments terminate at a half-round cartouche of shells on broad leaves at the rear, painted by John R. Penniman. The top is outlined by "rope" stringing and cross-banding of rosewood. The facing edge is set with a broad stringing of conjoined arrows. The beauty of its design makes this an extremely important piece of American furniture.

The Museum owns Thomas Seymour's bill for the commode to Mrs. Elizabeth Derby which reads, in part: "Large Mahogany Commode, $80.00. Paid Mr. Penniman's bill for painting shells on top of D° $10.00. . . ." The commode remained in the Derby family until given to the Museum by Miss Martha C. Codman (Mrs. Karolik). (H.H.S.)

FRANCISCO DE GOYA Y LUCIENTES. *Allegory of Spain, Time and History.*

The *Allegory of Spain, Time and History* is painted according to a tradition favored by many painters, including Tiepolo. Here Goya substitutes the figure of Spain for that of Truth, so that the allegory assumes a political significance. It is probably a polemical allusion to the hated minister Godoy, a favorite of the Queen, in the hope that Spain would follow France's example of reform. Spain, unclothed, appears in all her majesty under a brilliant celestial light, held by the hoary figure of Winged Time who flies beside her, hourglass in hand. At her feet, History, seated on a stone, records the event for posterity, while in the background bats and owls, symbols of wickedness and falsehood, flee into the darkness. (G.L.M.)

FRANCISCO DE GOYA Y LUCIENTES
Fuendetodos 1746 — Bordeaux 1828
Allegory of Spain, Time and History
Oil on canvas; 16 1/2″ × 12 3/4″.
27.1330
Gift of Mrs. Horatio Greenough Curtis
in memory of
Horatio Greenough Curtis.

EUGÈNE DELACROIX. *The Entombment.*

In *The Entombment,* Delacroix displays the full power of his mature dramatic style. In its expression of profound tragedy and despair, the painting is comparable to the celebrated masterpiece of his early years, *The Massacre of Scio.* The artist's stylistic individuality is based on strong contrasts of light and shade, passages of brilliant color, and fluid, instinctive brushwork. These technical means Delacroix placed at the command of his romantic soul, which thus often found expression in paintings of deep mood. Here the desolation of the group of mourners in the foreground, gathered about the body of Christ removed from the Cross, is intensified by the somber, empty landscape, the lowering sky, and the deep brooding shadows that envelop the figures. The low key of the composition provides a foil for the dramatic white shroud of Christ and the scarlet cloak of St. John. (P.T.R.) .

EUGÈNE DELACROIX
Charenton-Saint-Maurice 1798 — Paris 1863
The Entombment (1848)
Oil on canvas; 63 1/2″ × 51 1/2″.
96.21
Gift by contribution in memory
of Martin Brimmer.

JEAN-BAPTISTE CAMILLE COROT
Paris 1796 — Paris 1875
Girl with a Pink Shawl
Oil on canvas; 26 1/4″ × 21 1/2″.
19.81
Gift of Martha B. Angell.

JEAN–BAPTISTE CAMILLE COROT.   *Girl with a Pink Shawl.*

The paintings that brought Corot popular acclaim in the second half of his career — the·landscapes with feathery trees bathed in poetic light — are now the least regarded of his *oeuvre*. The paintings that never left his studio during his lifetime — the figure pieces of girls in costume — are today held in highest esteem. For a studio piece, *Girl with a Pink Shawl* is uncommonly objective. The painting is primarily an exercise in color and composition — and is left unfinished. Thus, it brings us into close contact with Corot's approach and method. It also shows that, however objective his intentions, he could not escape the innate lyricism of his nature. (P.T.R.)

GUSTAVE COURBET.   *The Quarry.*

Courbet was the champion of Realism. With his passionate love of the
physical world, he had no tolerance for the fantasies of the romantics or the

GUSTAVE COURBET
Ornans 1819 — La Tour-de-Peilz 1877
The Quarry (1857)
Oil on canvas; 83″ × 71″.
Originally the composition was shorter, coming within a few inches of Courbet's head. Adverse criticism after the first display of the painting in the Salon of 1857 persuaded him to heighten the picture and add a strip six inches wide on the left side. The first painting by Courbet to come to America, it was purchased by a group of young Boston artists in 1866.
18.620
Henry Lillie Pierce Fund.

conventions of the classicists. Consequently, untamed nature figures promi-
nently in his painting — animals, forests, rocky streams, rugged landscapes,
the sea. With unequalled directness and force, he painted the bulk and
texture of matter. Courbet loved the hunt and often followed the hounds in
his native Jura mountains. He had an appetite for its sights, smells and
sounds. In *The Quarry* he has painted himself with the dead stag, leaning
with satisfaction against a forest tree. Awaiting the arrival of the huntsmen,
he observes the growling hounds, while listening to the long note of the
hunting horn. (P.T.R.)

EDOUARD MANET.   *The Street Singer.*
The inspiration for this painting was Manet's accidental viewing of a Paris
street singer. The originality of using a casual subject and Manet's approach
to it are characteristic of the artist, and indeed of all the Impressionists, with
whom Manet was allied. In his belief that art could be created from the
humblest material and in his attitude of objectivity, Manet brilliantly as-
serted his opposition to the powerful Academic conventions of the day and
the taste that prevailed in the *salons*. The ultimate subject of *The Street
Singer* is Manet's consummate artistic instinct. (P.T.R.)

EDOUARD MANET.   *The Execution of the Emperor Maximilian.*
The tragic uselessness of the execution of Maximilian, death-blow to
France's political ambitions in Mexico, seems to have deeply impressed
Manet. In theme, composition and painterly technique, this painting shows
the influence of Goya's famous *Los tres de Mayo*. While the loose brush-

143

work and searing immediacy of the scene recall Goya's prototype, the flattened forms reflect an Oriental graphic style. The locked figures without faces define the episode with harsh realism. (G.L.M.)

EDGAR DEGAS. *The Duke and Duchess of Morbilli.*

In this magnificent portrait of the artist's sister and her husband, Degas' artistic heritage is clearly evident. He had studied in Italy during the previous decade and the influence of the Italian masters, especially Raphael, is still dominant. The perfect balance and felicitous proportioning of every element in the composition, which gives the painting a classic serenity, and the unaffected directness with which he presents the subjects reveal unmistakably the example of Raphael. Degas' admiration for Ingres can be seen in the refinement of drawing, the careful modelling, the generally smooth and painstaking technique. Yet there are signs pointing to the freer style of Degas' later period. The less than precise painting of the background passages and the "impressionistic" painting of the black gauze trimming of the Duchess' dress are hints of the brilliant, intuitive brushwork to come.

Degas' psychological perception dominates the portrait. The apprehensive and somewhat shy nature of his sister, and the proud, self-possessed character of his brother-in-law, a Neapolitan banker, are further accentuated by the brilliant positioning of the hands, which also serve to unify the two figures. As a study of human nature, as well as a flawless composition, *The Duke and Duchess of Morbilli* is one of Degas' great portraits. (P.T.R.)

EDGAR DEGAS.   *Carriage at the Races.*   *p. 145*
Degas began his career in the Academic tradition and, under the inspiration of Raphael and Ingres, created such great works as the *Duke and Duchess of Morbilli* (page 144). But contact with the painters of the new Impressionist movement and the influence of his friend and critic, Edmond Duranty, their champion, persuaded Degas to exhibit with them, though he would not join their movement. Among the first works that Degas created in response to the new association was *Carriage at the Races*. The painting appeared in the first Impressionist exhibition in 1874. For his "debut," Degas had created a little masterpiece. He was a colorist of rare distinction and in this work he refined his palette to a pearly softness: the gentle green of the course, the light blue sky dappled with little clouds, the evanescent pinks and yellows of the women's dresses and parasols. As a foil for this pastel harmony, the carriage and horses in the foreground are etched in crisp browns and blacks. While Degas resisted the loose brushstroke of his Impressionist friends, he nevertheless achieved their *plein-air* effect by his own means: the painting is bathed in delicate, diffused light. On the other hand, Degas adopted the informal subject matter of the Impressionists and shared their enthusiasm for Japanese principles of composition derived from the Ukioyoe wood-block prints then circulating in the non-Academic studios of Paris. The Japanese influence is apparent in the off-center placement of carriage and horses and the way in which they are arbitrarily cut at the bottom and right edges of the canvas. The bulldog on the carriage box, the pink rose behind the horse's ear, the horse's tail stirred by the breeze — all are witness to the freshness of Degas' eye. (P.T.R.)

THOMAS EAKINS.   *The Dean's Roll Call.*
In 1899 Eakins painted this portrait of Dr. James W. Holland, the noted urologist who held the chair of chemistry at Jefferson Medical College in Philadelphia. Dr. Holland later became dean of the college as well as professor of chemistry and toxicology. The spirited professor with his radiant face is depicted calling the roll of the graduating students at commencement, where the Hippocratic Oath was read and diplomas awarded.

Eakins surpassed every American painter, with the single exception of Copley, in his ability to penetrate the outward appearance of his subjects and express the psychological character beneath. He was also a shrewd observer of bodily movement and used it to heighten individuality. Certainly this is true of the Dean with his earnest face and tolerant eyes, and his habit

146

THOMAS EAKINS
Philadelphia 1844 — Philadelphia 1916
The Dean's Roll Call (1899)
Oil on canvas; 84″ × 42″.
43.211
Abraham Shuman Fund.

of throwing his head back and rocking on his heels. One feels that with Eakins every portrait was a serious and independent study, each requiring a totally different solution. In consequence, a distinct personality emerges with each likeness. Eakins was uncompromising in his scrupulous observation of fact, not the least of his detailed concern being the play of light on his subject. In this respect, and in his customary palette of rich, warm tones, he was influenced by Rembrandt. (P.T.R.)

JOHN SINGER SARGENT. *The Daughters of Edward Darley Boit.*
Edward Darley Boit was a Boston painter and a close friend of Sargent's. It was the habit of the Boit family to spend the winter in Europe and so it was in the drawing room of their Paris apartment that Sargent painted this famous group-portrait of the four Boit daughters. Sargent had been the brilliant pupil of the reigning French portrait painter, Carolus-Duran, and had established his studio in Paris. Precocious in his mastery of technique, Sargent was greatly influenced by Velázquez. He admired Velázquez' rich, dark palette, fluent brushwork, and, most important, his mastery of unconventional design. Sargent was patently conscious of Velázquez in the eccentric positioning of the young Misses Boit, crisply attired in white pinafores, in the shadowy hall of their home. The drama of the unexpected is pushed a step further by the accent of the immense blue and white Japanese vases in this "American *Las Meninas.*" (P.T.R.)

CLAUDE MONET. *Rouen Cathedral; Tour d'Albane, Early Morning.*
p. 150

Monet's fascination with catching in paint on canvas the endlessly changing and subtle effects of light and atmosphere reaches a climax in the famous series he painted of the façade of Rouen Cathedral. Monet's vantage point was a rented room above a shop across the square from the Cathedral. There, in the late winter of 1892 and 1893, he worked on the paintings at first hand. Most of the next year was spent in finishing the canvases in his studio at Giverny.

At many different hours of the day Monet disciplined his eyes so as to see not the object but rather the light that bathed it and the atmosphere between himself and the object. He rendered these effects with a fluid brush and an exquisite sense of color, guided by innate poetic feeling. The Rouen series is a particularly fascinating demonstration of Monet's devotion to the principles of Impressionism. For here in this Gothic monument is the extreme of solid reality that through Monet's eye and hand is transformed into an evanescent fantasy of light and color. (P.T.R.)

PIERRE AUGUSTE RENOIR. *Le Bal à Bougival.*
p. 151
The essence of Renoir's art is an easy and joyous response to life and to the sensuous beauty of the world. This happy attitude shines through every canvas — the opulent still lifes of flowers and fruit, the radiant landscapes of the *midi,* the scenes of holiday diversions, and the almost countless works devoted to the central theme of his *oeuvre,* women and children. *Le Bal à Bougival* is one of the masterpieces of Renoir's long career. It shows a young couple "lost" in each other's arms and moving with simple grace to the sen-

JOHN SINGER SARGENT
Florence 1856 — London 1925
The Daughters of
Edward Darley Boit (1882)
Oil on canvas; 7 1/4' × 7 1/4'.
19.124
Gift of Mary Louisa Boit,
Julia Overing Boit, Jane Hubbard Boit and
Florence D. Boit in memory of
their father.

149

CLAUDE MONET
Paris 1840 — Giverny 1926
Rouen Cathedral:
Tour d'Albane,
Early Morning (1894)
Oil on canvas;
41 3/4″ × 291 /8″.
Purchase,
Arthur Gordon Tomkins
Residuary Fund.

PIERRE AUGUSTE RENOIR
Limoges 1841 — Cannes 1919
Le Bal à Bougival (1883)
Oil on canvas; 70 3/4″ × 1/2″.
37.375
Anna Mitchell Richards Fund.

suous measure of the waltz. The smooth dynamics of the design, the charming subject, hold the eye and mind enthralled. One easily traces the amorous pursuit of the straw-hatted young man in the inclination of his head, while the downward glance of his beguiling partner speaks of her shy compliance. The message of young love, so naturally and yet so subtly expressed, is irresistible.

Renoir has framed the young woman's face in a red bonnet to make it the focal point of the picture, while the young man's dark blue suit provides a foil for the nacreous pink folds of the dancer's dress. A few adroit details provide the *mise en scène:* the gay companions with their glasses of beer at a table in the background, even the crushed cigarette beneath the dancer's swirling skirts. Renoir's art was strongly affected by the outlook of his close friends, Monet and Sisley, both Impressionists. He adopted the Impressionists' view of subject-matter: casual subjects from daily life, in contrast to the lofty themes garnished with rhetoric favored by the Academy. From the Impressionists he also took his luminist palette, to describe the action of light in *plein-air.* (P.T.R.)

PAUL CÉZANNE.   *Mme. Cézanne in a Red Armchair.*
This magnificent portrait of the artist's wife and frequent model is a striking example of Cézanne's contribution to European painting: the structure of form and composition in terms of color. Basing his art upon the realism of Courbet, Cézanne's innate great sense of color was stimulated by the light Impressionist palette of Pissarro. But, in contrast to the casual compositions of the Impressionists, Cézanne presents his subjects as vigorously structured designs, in which color rather than line, or the massing of light and dark, plays the dominant role. This compact, powerful picture is crowded with the solid figure of Madame Cézanne and the red foil of the overstuffed chair in which she sits. Cézanne's new coloristic technique is brilliantly exemplified in the painting of the face and hands of Madame Cézanne, in which form is achieved by means of small areas of subtly related color. Madame Cézanne's patience as a model is conveyed in this work; she appears perfectly immobile. Cézanne was known to reprove her if she altered her pose: "Don't move!" he would cry, "apples don't!" (P.T.R.)

PAUL GAUGUIN.   *D'où venons-nous? Que sommes-nous?*
                 Où allons nous?   *pp. 154–155*
This monumental painting, generally considered Gauguin's masterpiece, was executed during the artist's second and longest stay in Tahiti, in 1897. Gauguin intended it as his last philosophical testament, his *summa* before his suicide attempt. Failing in health, nearly penniless, and spiritually dejected and pessimistic, Gauguin worked with feversh haste on the painting and completed it within a month. He claimed that he worked directly on the canvas without preliminary drawings, but there is evidence that it was the product of a long period of thought and preparation.

Fortunately, Gauguin's attempted suicide failed and he lived to write about the painting in letters. In one, dated July, 1901, to his friend Charles Morice, Gauguin drew a diagram explaining the general meaning of the

152

painting. On the right (*D'où venons-nous?*), the women, child, dog and symbols of spring represent the beginning of life; at the center (*Que sommes-nous?*), man questions the meaning of existence, reaching up to pluck the fruit of the tree of knowledge; on the left (*Où allons-nous?*), man's awareness is seen as essentially tragic. An old woman "close to death" symbolizes the end of life. She is resigned to her fate, resigned to physical and intellectual death. And, "a strange and stupid bird concludes the poem." The bird is a warning representing "the futility of words." "Behind a tree two sinister figures, wrapped in dun-colored clothing, near the tree of knowledge, inject their note of sorrow brought on by that very knowledge; in contradistinction, the simple beings are surrendering themselves to the joy of living, in a virgin nature that could be a paradise of human conception." Thus the mystery of birth, life, and death are explored, tempered by the fall of man from innocence. Gauguin wrote in a letter of March, 1899, to Andre Fontainas, "The idol in my picture is not there as a literary explanation, but as a statue; is perhaps less of a statue than the animal figures, and is also less animal, since it is one with nature in the dream I dream before my hut. It rules our primitive souls, the imaginary consolation of our suffering, vague and ignorant as we are about the mystery of our origins and our destiny."

Artistically, the painting reveals Gauguin at the height of his artistic power. His personal figure style and symbolic color are perfectly fused to express a grand philosophical ideal in a mood of great quiet and mystery. (P.T.R.)

VINCENT VAN GOGH. *The Postman Roulin.* p. 156

Not long after Van Gogh arrived at Arles in 1888, he met Roulin, the postman, who became his closest friend and is frequently mentioned in Van Gogh's correspondence. Van Gogh painted five likenesses of Roulin, head and shoulders only; this is the only large representation of the sitter. Van Gogh wished to infuse his subject with his own personal reaction and understanding. He wrote to his brother Theo, "I do not know if I can paint the postman *as I feel him* . . ." But the impact of Roulin's personality on Van Gogh is quite clear. One observes it in the aggressive posture of the post-

154

PAUL GAUGUIN
Paris 1848 — Marquesas Islands 1903
D'où venons-nous? Que sommes-nous?
Où allons-nous?
(*Where do we come from? What are we?*
Where are we going?)
Oil on burlap; 54 3/4″ ×147 1/2″.
The painting was exhibited in 1898 at the Galerie Vollard, Paris. It was purchased by Ambroise Vollard in 1901.
36.270
Purchase,
Arthur Gordon Tompkins
Residuary Fund.
Right: detail.

man's head, his direct and piercing gaze, his nervous hands.

In Paris, in 1887, Van Gogh had abandoned the subdued tonal palette of the Hague School and had adopted the coloristic ideas and characteristic brushstroke of the Impressionists. Hardly less important in the development of his mature style was the influence of Japanese prints. Their clear, flat color and simple, bold contours appealed to him as a means of achieving a new form of expression, a rugged and deliberately primitive expression. In consequence, he made the postman in this portrait a vigorous, rangy figure who fills the whole canvas. His uniform is a nearly solid blue accented with bright gold buttons, and as Sharaku would do, Van Gogh placed him against a plain contrasting ground. (P.T.R.)

HENRI DE TOULOUSE–LAUTREC. *A La Mie.*

Toulouse-Lautrec, reared as an aristocrat, became in his brief lifetime a satirical commentator on the cafe and music-hall life of Paris. He found his milieu in the brash, noisy and often sordid life of places of public entertainment. The most celebrated entertainers of his day were the inspiration of some of his greatest works, but he was equally fascinated by anonymous pimps, harlots and inebriates.

A prodigy who displayed artistic prowess at the age of seventeen, Lautrec easily mastered academic painting under Paris masters, but broke with this tradition to follow the symbolist doctrine of arbitrary color and expressive line. He developed a style of immense potency and distinction. Uncompromising truth to life, however ignoble and mean, motivated his observation. In *A La Mie,* the relationship of this sodden pair of degraded characters, with their dissolute faces and idle hands, their drunkenness and dishevelment, holds us spellbound as a psychological essay. (P.T.R.)

EDVARD MUNCH. *The Voice.*

The essential isolation of man runs like a leit-motif through the entire *oeuvre* of Edvard Munch, the great modern artist of Norway. His people seem separated one from another, as if by invisible walls. Probably no other artist has succeeded so well in expressing the anxieties and tensions of daily existence. Munch took great care with his settings in order to enhance the mood of his subject. In *The Voice,* the loneliness and melancholy of the woman is echoed by the pine woods, uninhabited, remote, and still. The midnight sun of the northern summer casts its column of pale, eerie light on the water.

Munch chastened and simplified his style, paring away the non-essentials and relying to the fullest extent on the expressiveness of color. He was influenced by Gauguin, the Symbolists, and the principles of the Japanese print-makers. (P.T.R.)

EDVARD MUNCH
Engelhaug 1863 — Ekely 1944
The Voice (1893)
Oil on canvas; 34 1/2″ × 42 1/2″.
59.301
Ernest Wadsworth Longfellow Fund.

PABLO PICASSO
Malaga 1881 —
Standing Figure (1908)
Oil on canvas; 59″ × 39 1/2″.
The painting is one of several works
related to *Three Women,* formerly in
the Shchukin Collection,
now in the Hermitage.
58.976
Juliana Cheney Edwards Collection.

PABLO PICASSO.   *Standing Figure.*

In the early twentieth century in Paris, the nerve center of advanced art, artists determined to express form and space recreated by the imagination, rather than copied from nature. In collaboration with Georges Braque, this search for a new language of visual expression led Picasso to the birth of Cubism in 1909.

Standing Figure expresses unmistakably the temper of Picasso's creative drive at this moment of vital transition. The bold, slashing strokes of his   159

brush create new forms that have a primitive power and roughness. Closely related to these strong projections achieved by color and line are the passages that create the element of space with which the figure is integrated. Behind Picasso's plastic intoxication lay two sources of inspiration, the art of Cézanne and the sculpture of primitive people. *Standing Figure* is full of the tension and excitement of discovery. One senses it in the dynamism of the design, the action of the artist's brush, the flashing color. (P.T.R.)

CONSTANTIN BRANCUSI. *The Golden Fish.*
Brancusi did not wish to render a fish, but, to use his own words, "the flash of its spirit," its essential shape. Attached by a pin to a polished steel disk, *The Golden Fish* revolves slowly, changing the direction of its floating movement at the slightest touch. Penetrated by light, its abstract shape and movement are mirrored in the reflected surface of the disk.

In his search for ultimate shape and movement, Brancusi was fascinated with the fish for many years. The first version of 1922 and the last of 1930 are carved in marble. The Boston *Fish* and three other brass versions vary slightly but significantly the size and proportions of the earlier marble. In perfection of design and craftsmanship as well as in the realization of light-reflecting floating movement, these dazzling metal objects surpass the marble versions. (H.S.)

160

CONSTANTIN BRANCUSI
Pestisani-Gory 1876 — Paris 1957
The Golden Fish
Signed and dated: C. Brancusi — Paris
— 1924.
The original rough-textured base
of the sculpture, carved by
the artist, is lost.
Polished brass and steel; 5″ × 16 3/4″;
Base diameter 5″ × 19 3/4″.
57.739
William Francis Warden Fund.

HISTORY OF THE MUSEUM
AND ITS BUILDING

Department of Asiatic Art. The history of this department has been covered in the Introduction. The department is divided into three sections: Far East (China, Japan, Korea); Middle East (Islamic Art); and India (including also Malaysia and Indonesia).

Department of Egyptian Art. Long before the Museum was even contemplated, the Boston intellect was exploring ancient civilizations. In 1833 John Lowell, Jr. purchased the first monumental Egyptian sculptures to come to America, which, four decades later, were given to the new Museum. Together with the Way Collection, given in 1872, the Lowell gifts formed the nucleus of the Museum's Egyptian Collection.

The new Museum subscribed to the activities of the Egypt Exploration Fund in London. The Fund delivered to Boston such rewards as three colossal Twelfth Dynasty monuments — the Papyrus column, the Palm Leaf column, and the Hathor head capitol.

By 1902 the Collection was large enough to warrant the establishment of a separate Department of Egyptian Art, the first in the country. A year later, Theodore M. Davis donated a remarkable group of New Kingdom objects from his excavations in the Valley of the Kings at Luxor. Then in 1905, the Museum started the Harvard University–Museum of Fine Arts Egyptian Expedition under Dr. George A. Reisner, the Museum's Curator of Egyptian Art. The expedition was to last 40 years, and bring the Museum the full range of Egyptian art from the pre-dynastic period (4000 B.C.) to the Late Period of Roman Egypt (30 B.C. to A.D. 324). The core of Reisner's contribution is the art of the Old Kingdom, the greatest in Egyptian history; and the Museum's collection in this period is surpassed only by Cairo.

The Museum's First Egyptian Gallery is dominated by the imposing, though fragmentary, alabaster statue of Mycerinus, builder of the Third Pyramid. While in no way comparable with the Sphinx in size, this image of the Pharaoh carries the distinction of being the only other larger-than-life, or monumental, sculpture surviving from the Old Kingdom. In the same gallery is the double portrait of *Mycerinus and His Queen,* probably the finest work outside Egypt.

Among the many other riches of the collection are the sensitive portrait bust in alabaster, perhaps of Prince Shepseskaf, the son of Mycerinus; five "reserve" heads; and the great painted limestone bust of *Prince Ankh-haf* of the fourth Dynasty, generally believed to be the oldest realistic portrait in existence.

A principal site that yielded great treasures to Dr. Reisner was the rock-cut tomb of the Middle Kingdom at Deir el Bersheh in upper Egypt. In the tomb of Djehuti-Nekht, he found the prince's wooden sarcophagus, decorated with what are considered the finest paintings of the Middle Kingdom and among the oldest paintings in existence.

In 1913 Dr. Reisner began a nine-year pioneering campaign in the Sudan, which revealed much of the unsuspected culture of the land of Kush (Ethiopia), Egypt's southern neighbor. The last series of excavations by the Harvard-Boston expedition in the Sudan were at Meroë on the west bank of the Nile between the fifth and sixth cataracts. The findings there bring Egyptian and Kushite history into the Christian era, and have produced the Museum's extensive collection of Meroitic jewelry, and such monuments as the colossal statue in black granite of King Aspelta.

The expedition was closed following the end of World War II, having achieved for the Museum an incomparable representation of the entire range of Egyptian art, and having provided an archival treasure of data and documents still being digested, studied and published, and still advancing man's knowledge of ancient Egypt.

In 1958 the Department assumed charge of the art of Ancient Western Asia. Although much smaller than the Egyptian Collection, it is of exceptional quality. There is a splendid and comprehensive series of cylinder seals, several of which are among the earliest acquisitions of the Museum. Contributions on the part of the Museum to jointly sponsored excavations in Iraq, Syria, and Iran have brought Boston such remarkable objects as the two early bronze statuettes from Tell Judeideh, the group of ivory carvings from Assyrian Nimrud, the Persepolis palace relief of the lion and bull, as well as a series of Sassanian plaster reliefs from Iran. Through the long continued interest and generosity of Edward Jackson and Mary Holmes, the Iranian material has been enriched by superb Luristan bronzes.

Classical Department. The formative years of the Classical Department were shaped almost entirely by one individual, Edward Perry Warren. From 1890 to 1910 Warren virtually cornered the European art market. He bought directly from collectors in the capitals of Europe and from peasant excavators in Greece. The result is a magnificent collection that encompasses the entire range of Greek, Roman, and Etruscan art.

The first objects of classical origin to arrive at the Museum were a collection of heads from the island of Cyprus, purchased in 1872 from General di Cesnola, who later became the first Director of the Metropolitan Museum in New York. Other gifts soon followed.

The Department of Classical Art was organized in 1887, with Edward Robinson as Curator. He was appointed Director of the Museum in 1902, and in 1905 resigned to become Assistant Director, and in 1910 Director of the Metropolitan Museum in New York.

Then came the Edward Perry Warren era. Warren augmented his own resources with money from the Museum in the form of bequests from Catherine Page Perkins, Henry Lillie Pierce, and Francis Bartlett. So free was Bartlett's gift of $100,000 that he did not even wish to be consulted as purchaser. Subsequently, in 1912, Bartlett gave the Museum the enormous sum of $1,350,000.

The combination of these forces brought to Boston a collection of early bronzes that is one of the greatest in the world and is unsurpassed in America. The collection of Greek vases, also established by Warren, has only one rival in America, the Metropolitan Museum in New York. Another great Warren discovery, acquired in 1898, was the *Gold Earring of the Winged Nike.* Perhaps Warren's proudest triumph was the acquisition of the so-called *Boston Throne,* a marble, three-sided relief. Equally famous are the Warren finds of two of the most beautiful marble heads that have survived from antiquity, both dating from the fourth century B.C.: the *Bartlett Head of Aphrodite,* and the *Head of a Goddess.*

Warren was equally sensitive to Roman art and his perception in this field is exemplified by the terra-cotta *Portrait of a Roman* from the first century B.C. Yet another Warren legacy is the art of the ancient gem cutter. Over the years he gathered an unequalled collection of ancient cameo and intaglio gems.

The post-Warren years in the department have not been

without their excitements and achievements, guided by such eminent classical scholars as Arthur Fairbanks, Lacey D. Caskey, George H. Chase, and Cornelius C. Vermeule. One such excitement in 1913 demonstrates that good luck as well as connoisseurship builds a great museum. Aboard a ship from Piraeus to Boston, a Museum friend and passenger was approached by a Cretan peasant. The immigrant's most precious possession was a cigar box filled with ivory and gold fragments. Thus the cigar box came to the Museum and from those fragments was reassembled the famous *Snake Goddess,* the most refined and precious object ever recovered from the ruins of the Minoan civilization. More recent acquisitions have extended the collection by adding such objects as the *Seated Headless Sphinx,* of about 530 B.C., which is perhaps the finest of several sphinx monuments surviving from that time. A number of brilliant acquisitions in the field of red-figure vases permit an extraordinarily comprehensive survey of work produced by the major painters of fifth-century Athens. Significant additions have also been made to the collection of Greek coins, which now numbers almost 10,000. It is certainly the choicest in America and one of the great numismatic collections of the world.

Textiles Department. The Boston Museum was founded in the heyday of New England's textile industry. The charter specifically referred to the application of arts to industrial life, and it is not surprising to find that the second work of art registered by the new Museum was a tapestry. As early as 1877 the Trustees authorized an expenditure of $2,000 for works of art "to be made with reference to the advancement of artistic design in the industries of Massachusetts."

Before the turn of the century, the Textile Study Room — including the original deposit of the Boston Athenaeum: a tapestry, silk weavings, embroideries, and ecclesiastical vestments — was formally opened to students. To this foundation was added in 1893 a treasure of the utmost importance, a seventeenth-century wool carpet from India, embodying a landscape with figures and mythological beasts.

The constancy and scholarship of an individual collector, Dr. Denman Ross, then began to nurture the growth of the collection. His 11,000 gifts were divided among every department of the Museum. Only the Asiatic Department received a larger bounty than the 4,006 gifts he made to the textile collection. His originality as a collector of textiles is manifested not alone by the quantity of his gifts but by their diversity. They came from Spain, Italy, France, England, India, China, Japan, Persia, and include remarkably fine and rare groups of both Coptic and Peruvian weavings and embroideries.

Two major collections of civil and ecclesiastical textile objects, including English and Continental embroideries, laces, and costumes were acquired in the past three decades from Mr. Philip Lehman and Miss Elizabeth Day McCormick. Gifts from other donors have given the Museum an outstanding assembly of costumes ranging from an embroidered waistcoat said to have belonged to England's Queen Elizabeth I to evening dresses by Dior and Balenciaga. Many of the costumes are American, complementing the Department's New England embroideries of the late seventeenth through the early nineteenth centuries.

Originally envisioned as a section of the Department of Western Art, Textiles became an independent department in 1930 with Miss Gertrude Townsend as the first curator, and Adolph S. Cavallo as the second curator. Today the Museum's textiles rank among the great collections of the world for their high quality and rarity.

The Department's tapestry weavings begin with fine examples woven in the eastern Mediterranean world in the first millennium of our era, and extend to Europe in the fourteenth to eighteenth centuries, with important examples from weaving centers in England, Flanders, France, Germany, Holland, and Italy. These include *Scenes from the Passion of Christ,* a wool and silk tapestry of Franco–Flemish origin from the late fifteenth century; the great *Creed* tapestry, woven in Brussels around the same time; a set of four pilaster panels woven in Rome during the height of the Baroque Period; and a well-preserved Boucher tapestry. The collection of Peruvian tapestries ranging from the second half of the sixteenth century through the eighteenth, is one of the finest and most comprehensive. The collection is supplemented by Peruvian weavings and embroideries dating from the pre-Christian era to the time of the invasion by Pizarro in 1531.

Department of Paintings. The first gifts in the history of the Museum — *Elijah in the Desert* by Washington Allston, a superb American painting; and a pair of French genre paintings, *Halt at the Spring* and *Returning from Market* by François Boucher — established immediately the American and European courses of the Museum's painting collections. The tandem development has continued ever since, the one gaining on the other during one generation, then giving way during the next generation.

The full panorama of American painting is represented — from the earliest provincial portraits of Boston Puritans through the nineteenth-century Romantic Period to Winslow Homer and his contemporaries, the emergence of the "Ashcan" School, and the postwar reach to abstract expressionism and beyond. While nineteenth-century French art in the Museum forms one of the half dozen leading collections in the world, all schools are represented, from the eleventh century to the present day. The painting of the earlier European schools of Italy, Spain, Venice, and the Netherlands, is especially well represented. Spanish works begin with a twelfth-century Catalonian frescoed apse and continue to a group of major works of the sixteenth and seventeenth centuries, dominated by El Greco and Velázquez. The Venetian tradition is outlined by such sixteenth-century masters as Titian, Tintoretto, Veronese and Lotto, and eighteenth-century artists like Guardi, Canaletto, and Tiepolo. The early art of other Italian schools includes works by Duccio, Barna di Siena, Giovanni di Paolo, Fra Angelico, and Fra Carnevale. Netherlandish painting is represented by famous works of Rogier van der Weyden and Lucas van Leyden, and such seventeenth-century masters as Rembrandt, Ruisdael, Rubens, and van Dyck. The Baroque and Rococo movements in France boast examples by Poussin, Claude Lorrain, Boucher, Fragonard, Lancret, and Chardin. The group of eighteenth-century English portraits by Gainsborough, Romney, Reynolds, and Lawrence are remarkable. Finally, the expanding collection of modern art is providing an ever broadening view of twentieth-century art movements.

When the Museum opened in 1876, it contained a brilliant array of American paintings, permanently deposited by the Boston Athenaeum and the City of Boston — portraits by Copley, Stuart, and Nagle; historical works by Trumbull and West; and the best known of all American paintings, the Athenaeum portraits by Stuart of George and Martha Washington. These portraits of patriots, soldiers, statesmen, and their proud womenfolk, form a pantheon of American art.

Pride in American accomplishment has shaped the collection. The Museum began early to collect Winslow Homer: *The Fog Warning* was purchased in 1894; *All's Well* in 1899. John Singer Sargent, a Bostonian in spirit, was a favorite of the Trustees. They bought forty-five of his watercolors in one package in 1912; acquired by gift or purchase twenty-one paintings; and finally commissioned him to decorate the entrances to the Museum with his murals in 1916 and 1921.

Whistler is strongly represented as well as the post-Homer American artists Eakins, Ryder, and Cassatt. The Eight were overlooked during their years of rebellion against the Academy, and the first work of the group, a Henri, was not acquired until 1932. Now all are part of the collection, with special emphasis on Maurice Prendergast, the only Boston member of the Group. Nearer to our time, examples of the realists and expressionists have been acquired: Hopper, Sheeler, Hartley, Avery, Marin, and Feininger. The collection has been brought up to date in the most recent years by the work of such artists of fantasy as Lee Gatch, Loren MacIver and Jan Cox; and such leading masters of pure abstraction as Kline, Okada, Albers, and Morris Louis.

For years it was the academic and intellectual fashion to ignore American painting between Stuart and Homer, and dismiss the nineteenth century as a "barren" period. Fortunately for the Museum, and for American art, a champion of these years emerged in Maxim Karolik. He systematically and energetically discovered the creativity of this period. His gift in 1949 of the M. and M. Karolik Collection of 223 pictures was augmented by subsequent gifts and his ultimate bequest of 101 more works. His "rediscoveries" of both obscure and once-famous artists brought back into focus the Hudson River School and related landscape, portrait, still-life, and genre paintings, as well as half-forgotten artists of the West like Bierstadt.

The Boston painter William Morris Hunt, studying with Thomas Couture in Paris, encountered Millet and the Barbizon School, and was captured by Courbet and Corot. The first Courbet in America, *La Curée*, came to Boston in 1866 and was acquired by the Museum in 1918. Hunt also championed Millet, whose socialist realism shocked the Paris bourgeoisie but found a ready response in democratic America. Quincy Adams Shaw bequeathed more than sixty Millet paintings and pastels — including "The Sower" — to the Museum at his death in 1917.

It was only a step from the realism of Courbet to that other supreme invention of the French — Impressionism. Again a Boston painter, Lilla Cabot Perry, led the way. Mrs. Perry was enchanted by the work of Monet. Bostonians were again the target for this individual enthusiasm, and today the Museum possesses thirty-four works by this master dating from 1867 to 1908. The other Impressionists were equally admired by Bostonians and the Museum collection includes eight Pissarros, six Sisleys, and nine Degas. The familiar *Jockeys*, which the Trustees bought in 1903, was very likely the first Degas to be acquired by an American museum. Renoir was another favorite. *Le Bal à Bougival*, perhaps the best loved Renoir in America, is one of nineteen Renoirs in the Museum.

Coached by Mary Cassatt, the J. Montgomery Sears assembled a brilliant collection, which brought Manet's *The Street Singer* to the Museum. Robert Treat Paine II gave Boston not only the Degas *Duke and Duchess of Morbilli*, but the universally-loved *The Postman Roulin*, one of the five Van Gogh's in the Museum, and the magnificent *Madame Cézanne in a Red Arm Chair* by Cézanne. Denman W. Ross, who divided more than 11,000 gifts among all the departments of the Museum, contributed three Monets as early as 1906. On his death, John T. Spaulding left almost 100 paintings to the Museum, including two Cézannes, two Gauguins, a Lautrec, and Renoir's delightful *Children on the Seashore*, a superb Redon, *Flowers in a Green Vase*, and Van Gogh's *Berceuse*, a portrait of the wife of the postman Roulin.

Despite their susceptibility to French taste, Bostonians did not neglect the Old Masters. Perhaps the first painting of universal significance to arrive at the Museum was Rogier van der Weyden's *St. Luke Painting the Virgin*. It was the gift in 1893 of Henry Lee Higginson, founder of the Boston Symphony Orchestra, and thus Boston became the first American Museum to possess a

masterwork of the Flemish School. Even with such a strong beginning, the Northern schools were neglected in favor of the French and Italian schools. In 1962 the Flemish collection was enriched by the acquisition of a masterwork of the late fifteenth century — a perfectly preserved triptych, *The Martyrdom of Saint Hippolytus*, by a great but unidentified personality.

In contrast to certain other Departments of the Museum, where one or two towering figures have shaped the collection, the painting department has been molded by many personalities. John Singer Sargent was one. In 1903, he urged the Museum to purchase the El Greco portrait of the Trinitarian monk, *Fray Felix Paravicino*. By such means the Museum acquired the first El Greco in America. Sargent may also have been involved in 1901 with another great acquisition: the Velázquez portrait of *Don Carlos and His Dwarf*.

Boston has been fortunate in recent years to add to the Dutch Collection two types of painting in which the Dutch excelled — landscape and portraiture. *A Rough Sea* by Jacob van Ruisdael is a work of awesome beauty and immensity. Rembrandt's companion portraits of *Pastor Ellison and His Wife* are supreme, flawlessly preserved examples of his early oeuvre (1634). One final recent acquisition must be mentioned: the most distinguished work of Italian Mannerism in America, Il Rosso Fiorentino's *Dead Christ Flanked by Angels*.

Department of Decorative Arts and Sculpture. Decorative arts were one of the primary concerns of the Museum's founders in 1870. Their first public announcement included a proposal "to provide opportunities and means of instruction . . . with their industrial application through lectures, practical schools, and a special library." It was expected that examples of design and color would elevate the standard of taste and specifically "be of great service to all students of design and manufacturers." Although most of the accessions prior to 1893 consisted of plaster cast reproductions, the old Museum on Copley Square could already display Claude-Nicolas Ledoux' superb panels from the Hotel Montmorency in Paris, Charles C. Perkins' gifts of Italian Renaissance sculpture, and George Wales' bequest of European ceramics.

By 1908, the growing collections of the Museum and the move to the new building on the Fenway dictated the need for classification. The Department of Western Art was accordingly constituted to include paintings, textiles, and other collections that were primarily examples of decorative arts. These "other collections" began to take on a life of their own and, in 1919, the Trustees purchased their first interior of an American home. . . ." Under the direction of Edwin J. Hipkiss, an assembly of rooms and galleries was installed with objects of the same period and national origin. A new wing was built to accommodate this sequence of period rooms, and it was formally-opened in 1928 as the new Department of Decorative Arts of America and Europe.

The new wing added 50 galleries on three floors to the Museum's exhibition space. The installations were created in the firm belief that where works of art, both major and minor, were made to be seen together in their own day, they are best seen together in our day. These period rooms included a Louis XVI Salon from Paris, a Tudor Room from Somerset, England, and three McIntire rooms from Essex County, Massachusetts. Galleries of silver, furniture, pewter, glass, and ceramics were interspersed with the period rooms, providing the visitor with more than 50 individual exhibitions.

The main emphasis of these years was placed on American art. In 1939, however, the Department broadened its scope with the arrival of Dr. Georg Swarzenski, the distinguished medievalist from Frankfurt, and General Director of Frankfurt's Municipal Museums. In the space of 15 years he assembled a medieval collection that has few rivals in America. Dr. Swarzenski vastly

164

enriched the Museum's collections, and developed the community's latent taste for medieval and later European styles. The medieval tradition in the Museum is given continuity by the present curator, Dr. Swarzenski's son, Hanns.

Time has modified the older ensemble theory of installation, and today the galleries convey the experience of artistic creation by emphasizing palpable and intimate personal contact with individual objects. This aim has, in turn, broadened the collecting policy to supplement the comprehensive collections of furniture, silver, and ceramics with both monumental statuary and precious small objects of the same period and spirit.

Since 1963 the department has been called the Department of Decorative Arts and Sculpture. In recent years, the Department has acquired such notable treasures as the early-thirteenth-century polychromed oak figure of the *Virgin and Child* from the Ile-de-France and the *Madonna of Victory,* signed and dated 1771 by Johann Martin Mutschele of Bamberg. Inspired realism in the sculpture collection is represented by six Houdon busts; one of George Washington, a fitting companion to the Stuart portrait in the Painting Department; and another of Thomas Jefferson, the most vivid and convincing of his life-portraits in sculpture. In contrast, inspired abstraction appears in the beautiful polished brass and bell-metal *Fish* of Constantin Brancusi.

The European Decorative Arts range from the early Middle Ages to the nineteenth century. Outstanding examples from the early medieval and Romanesque periods are the eleventh-century Crucified Christ from Salzburg and the twelfth-century enamelled plaque depicting the Three Worthies in the Fiery Furnace. From the Late Gothic and the Romanesque periods: stained glass from Hampton Court, Harefordshire; the small Donatello relief of the *Madonna of the Clouds;* ten della Robbias including Luca's *Madonna of the Niche;* a collection of Hafner Ware, among them a unique portrait bust. From the Baroque and Rococo periods: an outstanding group of religious and secular South German and Austrian carvings in wood and stone; faience and porcelain including one of the masterpieces of animal sculpture, a Meissen monkey with the mark of Augustus the Strong.

Among the first gifts to the Museum was eighteenth-century French furniture from the collections of Colonel Swan and Edward Deacon. In 1965 the late Forsyth Wickes bequeathed his superb collection of eighteenth-century French art in its entirety to the Museum. The bequest included over 800 objects — furniture, porcelains, paintings, and drawings.

The collection of modern sculpture is slowly but systematically developing and now includes works by Rodin, Gauguin, Henry Moore, Reg Butler, Calder, Giacometti, and George Rickey.

The American and English Arts sequences display the venerable holdings of greater Boston's church silver; and the finest work of New England's silversmiths, with an unmatched collection of Revere silver that includes the famous "Liberty Bowl." Equally distinguished is the extensive collection of English silver beginning with the Elizabethan Age, which was made possible by the Frank Brewer Bemis bequest and the Theodore Wilbour Fund. The M. and M. Karolik Collection of American Furniture is unparalleled and is supplemented with masterpieces by the leading cabinetmakers of New England, New York, and Philadelphia.

Department of Prints and Drawings. The oldest of the Museum Departments, the Print Department was organized on February 1, 1887, and placed in the receptive hands of Sylvester R. Koehler. He took charge of 4,151 prints in the Museum and the Gray Collection of 5,145 prints belonging to Harvard College. With this founda-

tion, Koehler indefatigably mounted exhibitions — including the first major American showing of Rembrandt's etched work; wrote catalogues; and relentlessly importuned the Trustees for funds and resources. So total was his commitment that on his death in 1900, he bequeathed his own collection to the Museum.

When Harvard, as expected, withdrew its Gray and Randall collections, Koehler redoubled his acquisitive efforts. He persuaded the Trustees to buy the Sewall Collection with funds bequeathed by Harvey D. Parker. The collection contained about 23,000 prints, covering the wide field of graphic art over four centuries. The purchase set off a chain reaction of gifts and support, notably from Francis Bullard and his family, directed towards the acquisition of master prints. During this early period, the Department published "The Print Collector's Quarterly," the only English language periodical devoted to "awakening and gratifying the taste for fine engraving."

Under Emil H. Richter, the second curator, and his successors, FitzRoy Carrington and Henry P. Rossiter, the collections were vastly increased. The uneasy peace between two world wars enabled the curators to buy wisely and economically in London and Europe to the aggrandizement of the print collection.

Henry P. Rossiter, the fourth curator, who served from 1923 to 1967, was universally known with affection and respect as the Dean of American print curators. He built nobly on the splendid tradition he had inherited, and stamped the hallmark of independence on his collecting policy. He bought, for example, seventeenth-century Dutch prints by less well-known masters and chiaroscuro woodcuts and very early lithographs that are among the most important in any print room. Well ahead of other connoisseurs was his acquisition of a virtually complete collection of etchings by the French Mannerist, Jacques Bellange. A special enthusiasm of his was the generally overlooked and prodigious output of English book illustrators of the 1860's. In 1965 he purchased the finest impression of Goya's rare masterwork, *Colossus.* He instituted the conservation laboratory of the Department — perhaps the oldest, and certainly the most experienced establishment of its kind in the country. Today, the Department is in the hands of the fifth curator, Eleanor Sayre, a world authority on Goya.

The collection of Old Master drawings is small but distinguished and constantly growing. The assembly of books, containing a rich variety of work by the great illustrators of each school and period, is particularly strong in the French eighteenth century. The watercolors by William Blake include a series for *Paradise Lost,* the *Plaques,* and Milton's *Comus.* Second to none are the representations of nineteenth-century American watercolors and drawings (the M. and M. Karolik Collection) by Homer, Sargent, Prendergast, and Hopper.

The great distinction of the Department lies in its extensive print collection. Engravings by German, Italian, and Netherlandish masters are impressive and include Schongauer, Stoss, Dürer, Pollaiuolo, Mantegna, von Leyden, van Dyck, and Rembrandt. French printmakers include Callot, Daumier, the Barbizon School, and the Impressionists. The thrust and change of the twentieth century is universally documented in color and black and white. Nor should it be forgotten that the range of the chiaroscuro print from the early sixteenth century through the eighteenth is without peer in the world; that the lithograph, the ornament print, and the portrait are areas of great strength; and that the collection of prints from Turner's *Liber Studiorum* is on a par with that of the British Museum and is accompanied by a striking group of his watercolors and drawings.

More than 300,000 objects are currently registered in the Department which began 82 years ago with less than 5,000 examples, attracting but 14 visitors its first year to examine prints not on exhibition.

THE BUILDING

The Museum of Fine Arts, Boston, was founded on February 4, 1870, as a private institution managed by a board of trustees, both appointive and elective. Its resources included the art collections of the Boston Athenaeum, a proprietary library; a collection of engravings, since withdrawn, from Harvard College; a collection of architectural casts from the Massachusetts Institute of Technology.

The first building, a Ruskinian Gothic structure on land given by the City of Boston in the newly-filled Back Bay, opened its doors on the first centennial of the Declaration of Independence, July 4, 1876. Despite two additions to the main building, financed by public subscription, the Copley Square location proved inadequate by reason of the growing collections, and the overbuilding of the adjacent area. In 1899, the trustees, therefore, bought twelve acres of

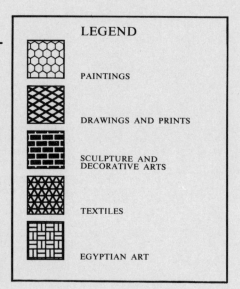

LEGEND

PAINTINGS

DRAWINGS AND PRINTS

SCULPTURE AND DECORATIVE ARTS

TEXTILES

EGYPTIAN ART

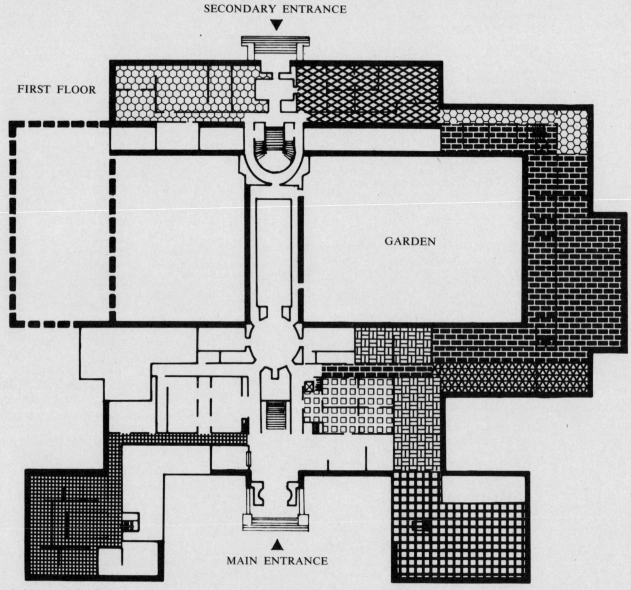

SECONDARY ENTRANCE

FIRST FLOOR

GARDEN

MAIN ENTRANCE

The unmarked areas include offices, reading rooms, restoration rooms, and rooms with recent acquisitions. Other parts of the Museum are in the process of expansion or reorganization.

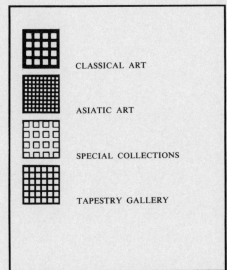

CLASSICAL ART

ASIATIC ART

SPECIAL COLLECTIONS

TAPESTRY GALLERY

land in the Fenway, a major element of the Boston park system designed by Frederick Law Olmsted, and financed the new building by sale of the property in Copley Square (now the Sheraton Plaza Hotel) and public subscription. Guy Lowell was retained as the architect to design a Neo-Classical structure, whose elaborate façade concealed a carefully designed and extremely practical interior. The building opened to the public on November 15, 1909. A central wing and the Robert Dawson Evans galleries for paintings on the northwest Fenway side were added in 1915; a separate building for the School of the Museum was built to the southwest in 1927; and a wing for Decorative Arts was added to the southeast end of the building in 1928. The building thus contained seven structurally separated departments in 178 galleries. Under the impetus of the Centennial Program, the Museum has constructed two additions at the southeast end of the Museum, and a new service wing at the southwest end which will eventually be complemented by an additional sequence of galleries. This construction program, begun in 1966, will increase the size of the Museum by 50 per cent.

SECOND FLOOR

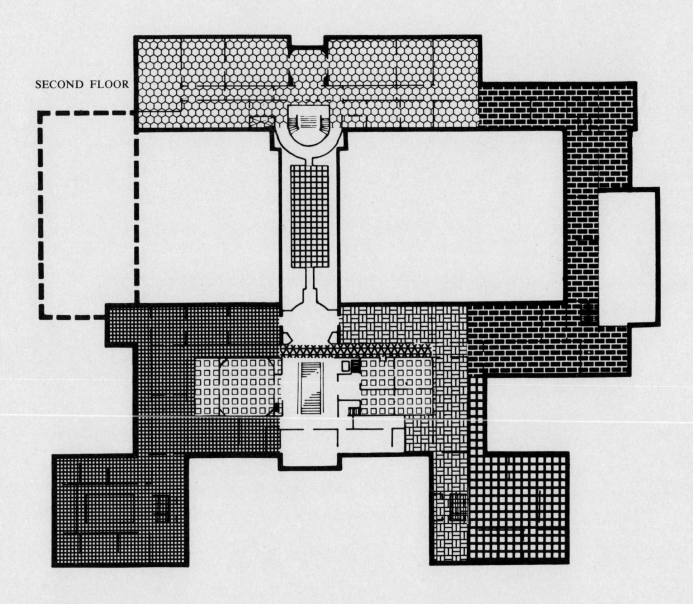

SELECTED BIBLIOGRAPHY

American Paintings in the Museum of Fine Arts, Boston. 2 vols. (Boston, 1969).

Boston Museum Bulletin. Boston, 1903–

BUHLER, KATHRYN C. *American Silver in the Museum of Fine Arts, Boston.* 2 vols. (Boston, 1970).

CAVALLO, ADOLPH S. *Tapestries of Europe and of Colonial Peru in the Museum of Fine Arts, Boston.* 2 vols. (Boston, 1968).

COMSTOCK, MARY B. and VERMEULE, CORNELIUS C. *Greek, Etruscan and Roman Bronzes in the Museum of Fine Arts, Boston.* (Boston, 1969).

DUNHAM, DOWS. *The Egyptian Department and Its Excavations.* (Boston, 1958).

Greek, Etruscan & Roman Art: The Classical Collections of the Museum of Fine Arts, Boston. rev. ed. (Boston, 1963).

HIPKISS, EDWIN J. *Eighteenth-Century American Arts: The M. and M. Karolik Collection.* (Cambridge, Mass., 1950).

Illustrated Handbook. (Boston, 1964).

M. and M. Karolik Collection of American Paintings: 1815 to 1865. (Cambridge, Mass., 1949).

M. and M. Karolik Collection of American Water Colors & Drawings: 1800–1875. 2 vols. (Boston, 1962).

Museum of Fine Arts, Boston: Oriental Art. (Boston, 1969).

Museum of Fine Arts, Boston: Western Art. (Boston, 1970).

RANDALL, JR., RICHARD H. *American Furniture in the Museum of Fine Arts, Boston.* (Boston, 1965).

RATHBONE, PERRY T. *The Forsyth Wickes Collection.* (Boston, 1968).

SALDERN, AXEL VON. *Ancient Glass in the Museum of Fine Arts, Boston.* (Boston, 1968).

SMITH, WILLIAM STEVENSON. *Ancient Egypt as Represented in the Museum of Fine Arts, Boston.* 6th edition, revised. (Boston, 1968).

TSENG, HSIEN-CH'I and DART, ROBERT PAUL. *The Charles B. Hoyt Collection in the Museum of Fine Arts, Boston.* Vol. 1. (Boston, 1964).

For their courtesy in furnishing information of great value for the preparation of this book, we wish to thank Perry T. Rathbone, Jan Fontein, Patricia Alward and Carl Zahn of the Museum of Fine Arts.

INDEX OF ILLUSTRATIONS

INDEX OF NAMES

Note: Italic numbers refer to names mentioned in captions.

GENERAL INDEX